Build the Right Thing

How to build high-growth agile digital businesses customers love

by
HAJA J DEEN

Acknowledgements

Writing a book is harder than I thought and more rewarding than I could have ever imagined. None of this would have been possible without my wife, Sameema, and my lovely daughters Farihah and Faizah, who kept me motivated despite me taking up most of our Saturdays with writing.

I'm eternally grateful to my mother and father who taught me and continually remind me of patience and perseverance without which this book would never have been completed.

It has been a huge blessing to have had some amazing experiences and learnings during my roles in both startups and gigantic businesses across the world. A very special thanks to Dr. Tan Huat Chye of Fast-Foods.net for believing in me to build cutting-edge technology way ahead of its time, Naoshi Yoshida of NTT for teaching me the people aspects of technology, Tetsuro Mikami of NTT for guiding and mentoring me to drive innovation through large organizations, and Peter Hindle and David Fenton of Saint-Gobain UK for believing in me to lead the digital transformation of a multibillion pound turnover business.

A timely meeting with the Govtech Singapore's team lead to the Moments of Life case studying being featured in the book. My sincere appreciation to Ping Soon Kok and Dominic Chan.

Assembling this book has been an exercise in forming a global team of true experts in book publishing, thanks to various digital talent marketplaces. I am truly thankful for the wonderful team that worked on making this book happen. Jo-Finchen-Parsons from the

UK (Reedsy) for editing and guiding me to make this work much better than it would have ever been, Ivan Butler from the UK (Freelancer) for editing and proofreading, Dinnah from Bosnia Herzegovina (99 Designs) for her illustration that adorns the book cover, Ruchi Rani from India (Upwork) for patiently drawing the diagrams within the book, Davor Nikolic from Serbia (Fiverr), who amazed me with his typesetting and layout skills, and Christian Freed from the US (Fiverr) for editing the book summary.

To all the individuals I have had the opportunity to work with, lead, be led by, or watch their work from afar, I want to express my gratitude to you for being an inspiration for *Build the Right Thing*.

Last but not least, writing a book was never on my to-do list. A greater force than me gave the inspiration, orchestrated the myriad circumstances that led to the contents within this book, and brought together the right people at the exact right time to manifest this book that is now in your hands. Through this book our paths have crossed briefly, and for that I am truly grateful.

Contents

Acknowledgements   iii
INTRODUCTION   1
  Why I Wrote This Book   1
  A Blueprint for Success   3
  But What About Lean?   5
  The Benefits of a Blueprint   8
  Who Is This Book For?   10
  How to Use This Book?   17
  Why Plan?   19

Chapter 1
Where Do You Compete?   23
  From Clarity to Confidence   23
  Which Sector Are You In?   25
  The Industry—Your Real Playground   25
  Which Niche Are You Targeting?   27
  What Are the Profitable Segments Within Your Niche? 30
  Timing Your Entry   31
  Resources   34

Chapter 2
How Do You Compete?   37
  Target Customer Segment   40
  Target Customer Persona   42
  Current Customer Journey (and Pain Points)   46
  Your Unique Solution   53
  Homegrown Customer Journey   60
  Ideal Customer Journey (Underpinned by
  Simplified Operations)   62

TransferWise: Fintech Star Reimagining Money Transfers   62
Resources   65

Chapter 3
What Resources Do You need?   69

Chapter 4
Agile Mindset   73
Clarity   74
Transparency   79
Long-Term Thinking   84
Energizing Behaviors   85
Resources   94

Chapter 5
Agile Team   96
Team Foundations   102
Customer Centricity   104
Living Agile   105
Startup Teams   110
Corporate Digital Transformation and New
Venture Teams   118
Teams for Scale-Ups   126
Playing a Team Game   128
Resources   130

Chapter 6
Agile Technology   133
Why Every Modern Entrepreneur Needs to
Grasp Technology   134
The Three Key Technology Platforms You Need   135
Agility Through Continuous Integration   143
A Simple Method to Filter the Technology Noise   145
How to Develop Your Product   148
Resources   153

Chapter 7
GovTech Singapore – Moments of Life   155

Chapter 8
Conclusion   164

INTRODUCTION

Why I Wrote This Book

At 11 p.m. on a Saturday night in 1999, there I was sitting at my office desk in a Singapore business park, finishing another week of software development. After another 90-hour week at work I wasn't tired or worn out but rather exhilarated. I walked the short distance to grab a taxi and reflected on the journey the business had taken over the last six months.

Just six months prior, Fast-Foods.net had been an unknown start-up based in Singapore. I'd joined the two founders of the company as a co-founder, tasked with helping to develop the web-based software required to run the website. Even the process of joining the team was an 'agile' experience, characteristic of startups. To supplement my day job, I posted a classified ad offering my services as a software developer, specializing in ColdFusion. In response, one of the founders of Fast-Foods.net immediately offered me a full-time role to build their web-based platform.

The idea was fairly simple: Fast-Foods.net was a website that allowed users to order takeaways from quick-service restaurants such as Pizza Hut and KFC. Today this seems nothing remarkable, but in 1999 this was an innovative novelty and quite remarkable.

Within six months the business had expanded to three countries, with over 50,000 users registered and ordering food on the platform. The business had already raised more than S$2 million and was poised for further growth. The team had grown to more than 50 people; my own team had expanded to seven people, all working together on the system. And it was succeeding. On the day of the Singapore press launch, we took out a full-page advertisement in the main newspaper. Within 24 hours, there were over 20,000 registrations on the website. The traffic had exceeded our wildest expectations; so much so that we had to restart the server to keep handling the load!

Now, reflecting on the journey the business had taken, it occurred to me that the success and growth of Fast-Foods.net could be attributed to a few characteristics. Firstly, the entrepreneurs who founded it understood their customers and their needs, and offered a proposition that was far superior to ordering a takeaway over the phone. Leveraging the power of the web simply made the whole process easier for the customer and was a game changer in the market. Secondly, the founders instilled their vision in the team, meaning they were able to attract, motivate, and retain the right talent to achieve that vision. The expansion resulted in new offices in Hong Kong, and I was tasked with opening the Tokyo office.

Though I didn't know it at the time, that was the peak of the company's success. Fast-Foods.net stopped operations just after the dot-com burst of 2000. Even though there was significant traction, the Nasdaq crash and ensuing near disappearance of venture funding meant that we couldn't raise the additional funding required to stay in business. Today, as I write this book and witness the success of similar concepts, such as Just Eat, Uber Eats, and many others in the same space, the sound rationale for Fast-Foods.net is blatantly obvious, but it came too early. In my view, Fast-Foods.net was a resounding success, even though it didn't get a multibillion tech startup exit, because it had succeeded in attracting significant numbers of customers and it was truly innovative.

Since then I've always wondered what it would take to consistently reproduce the success and potential of Fast-Foods.net in another new venture. After two decades and an international career in both the corporate and startup world (spanning project managing software development, digital strategy, and team build outs), plus a full-time MBA, I've developed the blueprint for digital startup success that I will share in this book.

Build the Right Thing is the result of two profound realizations:

If you build the right thing instead of focusing on building things right, customers will love what you have built, and everything else becomes easier.

To build the right thing you need a step-by-step blueprint to reach clarity for yourself and convince others to help you build it and grow it.

A Blueprint for Success

This blueprint for success is the product of analyzing more than 20 projects from startups and large corporations alike. These projects have comprised both wild successes and dismal failures. I'm now convinced there is a reliable framework that any entrepreneur or intrapreneur can use to significantly improve the chances of achieving the goals of their new venture.

In the case of Fast-Foods.net, the two founders were inquisitive entrepreneurs determined to create the next big, disruptive innovation. They understood that they needed to plan a solution starting with the customer in mind; their needs, triggers, and motivation. They realized that any entrepreneur starting a venture and thinking about where and how they want to compete, is risking failure if they don't focus on the customer. They understood they needed to build the right thing instead of trying to build things right.

Too often we look at successful businesspeople and imagine that they have some extraordinary skills or talents that the rest of us lack. The media portray Jeff Bezos, Bill Gates, Elon Musk, etc. as super charismatic, with unending personal ambition. However, if we separate the people from what they have built, we can see that the success of Amazon, Microsoft, and Tesla is a result of providing an innovative service or product with the right mix of technology and talent at its heart. The founders have endowed their teams with the right mindset and culture, allowing them to execute the plan.

Fortunately, there is a predictable pattern to this mix of strategy, mindset, talent, and technology. Throughout the rest of this book, I've simplified this winning formula into a two-phase blueprint, which you can use to launch your own venture.

The blueprint for helping to 'build the right thing', which I call the 'Agile Digital Strategy Blueprint', helps you to think through five key areas—two in the planning phase and three on resources you need.

1. Plan
   a. Where do you compete?
   b. How do you compete?

2. Execute
   a. Agile Mindset
   b. Agile Teams
   c. Agile Technology

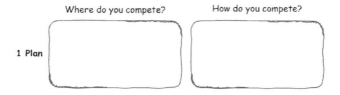

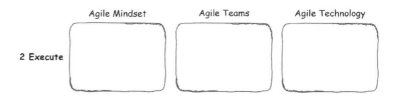

By the time you finish this book, you will have the knowledge and tools to:

- Confidently state your purpose regarding your product and its vision;
- Compete in a niche area by understanding your customers' journeys and your competitive advantage;
- Share your new vision to attract the capital, talent, and resources to execute it;
- Plan which resources you need in terms of mindset, people, and technology to execute and realize your plans; and

- Communicate continuously with your team, partners, and financiers to stay true to your vision, correct your course as needed, and reach your end goals.

Learning to convincingly communicate your vision to a team of people will greatly improve your chances of success. Without this ability, entrepreneurs miss out on the assistance of those who would be able to help them achieve their vision.

As the tools I provide in this book demonstrate, even complex ideas can be broken down into concepts that most can appreciate. When you assist people to properly understand your idea, with simple visuals, you maximize the chances that they will appreciate your idea and give it their full support. That is this book's mission: with the help of the templates to create your own blueprint, you will be able to produce a refined idea that is visual and easy to communicate and that most people can understand, so that they can either give you constructive feedback or support you with the resources you need to reach your goals.

So that you can build the right thing!

But What About Lean?

I understand why entrepreneurs are not the most likely to embrace a theoretical framework or fit their ideas into one, preferring action and learning through trialing. Entrepreneurs are naturally action oriented rather than theoretical.

The Lean approach of getting started quickly, rolling out beta products, getting customer feedback and reiterating, while sound in theory, often leads to failure when not built on a solid guiding vision and strategy. This approach creates quick confidence in the entrepreneur but, without clarity of purpose, confidence can take you in completely the wrong direction.

The blueprint I propose in this book helps you to reach clarity in days or weeks, rather than months. It refines your avenues of exploration and provides you with a toolkit to confidently communicate your planned idea. Essentially, the Lean approach answers the "How is it done?" question, and I'm a fan in the right circumstances. When executed upon the foundations of a strong vision, the Lean approach works, and I've witnessed it first-hand at Toyota, which is a great Lean success story. However, we need clarity on the 'Why?' and 'What?' before we get to the 'How?'

This agile digital strategy blueprint that I share with you creates clarity on the strategy and the agile resources you need to execute and deliver your strategy. Most importantly, the blueprint provides you with a simple visual framework to reflect on and fill out as you go through the chapters. By the end of the book you will have something exceptionally valuable: your own personal blueprint; one that you can share with others to attract capital, talent, and partnerships to achieve your vision.

In the following valuable example, you will see that while Toyota is famous for its use of the Lean approach, it also has something else that is less well known: clarity of purpose to which all employees are aligned.

Employees who are trusted to make appropriate decisions and who choose not to partake in office politics are the direct result of having clarity of purpose. But is this magic unique to Toyota or can it be reproduced elsewhere? Part of the behavior stems from the Japanese

Valuable Insights from Toyota

I saw Lean first-hand while executing a large Enterprise Resource Planning (ERP) analysis project for Toyota.

Toyota started its Vietnam operations in the early 1990s. Due to phenomenal car sales growth, within just a few years Toyota exceeded all forecasts and was nearing its ERP system capacity. The company I worked for was hired to analyze and upgrade Toyota's systems so that it could handle up to 100,000 cars per year. I was part of a team of 20 experts from Singapore, Japan, and Vietnam that handled this project over six months. This project was a highlight of my career. It was intense, working over 80 hours per week, but so rewarding, as I had the opportunity to work with some of the best minds I've come across in the corporate world.

Through my interactions with the employees of Toyota, it was obvious that they were driven by a very clear purpose. It wasn't displayed on any poster or in a long mission statement delivered by the CEO, but had been embedded in the culture and was readily adopted by all employees, permeating to every level. I learnt that this culture takes root within Toyota's people as they focus on one thing: the end customer's best possible experience. This focus shapes all decisions and behaviors: anything affecting production, sales, or customer service. It wasn't just the senior employees at the top of the organization who were behaving like this but everyone we met in the company. Everyone shared unspoken, common goals and behaviors. It was truly inspiring to see this culture in action, and even more inspiring to not find the inevitable office politics, pandering to decision-makers, and design by committee. This was Toyota's open secret - everyone there knew of its purpose, to delight customers, but no one spoke of it.

culture, work ethics, and beliefs. Through my experience of working internationally, for example with the Japanese telecommunications company NTT, I've learnt that culture plays a key role in shaping organizational behavior. Hence, I've taken care to ensure that the blueprint described in this book is valuable across any culture. What happens at Toyota, while not fully reproducible like for like in another organization, can be adapted and leveraged for success.

This is the key: before executing their plan using the agile approach, the people who work at Toyota already have a very clear vision of what they are trying to achieve. This understanding has helped me deliver numerous successful projects across the globe, always beginning with a very clear purpose about what I'm trying to give to my customers. Over time, I've honed this process and now I would like to share it with you in this book. Through this method, I will assist you to systematically think through your customers' needs and how you can serve them in a competitive way relative to the market. It is this customer-centricity and vision that draws teams together to behave in productive ways. Throughout this book, I will explain this process step by step.

The Benefits of a Blueprint

I've met many entrepreneurs who just throw caution to the wind and start building a product. When anyone says that planning and strategy is simply theory, my response normally is, "Gravity is theory too. However, anyone sensible wouldn't step off a cliff claiming that gravity is theory!" In the same way, any new startup or project is affected by the laws of economics, competition, and market forces. We compete with other providers for customers and we compete for talent and capital. Hence, leveraging these forces in the most effective way helps you, not just to understand where and how you are operating, but also to convince others to help you with capital and the resources you need to execute successfully.

The visual framework is your blueprint: the map with which you guide all others to follow you. If you are attempting anything worthwhile, you will need a team of backers, financiers, and builders to help you achieve. Having this well-thought-out map in your hand increases your credibility and attracts followers.

Nothing that significantly affects the world in a positive way is achieved by an individual alone. It is always through a team, no matter how small. It is my wish and hope that, through this book, you will discover the power of transmitting ideas clearly and in so doing mobilize teams around you. When you reach clarity on what you want and can catalyze others to help you achieve what you want, the world is waiting to reward you with all that you desire.

Talent wins games, but teamwork and intelligence win championships.

~ Michael Jordan ~

Who Is This Book For?

This book is useful for two groups of people. Firstly, entrepreneurs who are embarking on a new venture. Secondly, executives or managers involved in a new venture within an already established organization, that is, intrapreneurs. The principles in this book are equally useful to both groups. Importantly, the information and tools in this book are designed for those who want to take *action*. It isn't a theoretical exercise in thought experiments.

If you are an entrepreneur looking to refine your idea, attract capital, talent, and launch your product, then this book is for you. It will help you understand and clarify your business model and define your product offering in a very targeted way. The tools in this book will help you to communicate your proposition to your potential financial backers so they buy into your idea and support you with the resources you need to succeed. When you are further along in the journey and have launched your entrepreneurial venture, the concepts explained in this book will help you to sense check your model and accelerate your success by aligning your team to a simple, newly energized vision.

The second group of people who will find this book most useful are executives and managers in corporate organizations who are tasked with digitally transforming their organization or launching a new venture. My agile digital strategy blueprint will help you to clarify the target business model, convince the various stakeholders within your organization, and get the necessary resources approved so you can execute your plan. It will also be immensely useful in assisting you to communicate your project to future teammates and partners within your organization. This will encourage them to back you, or at least not stand in your way, so you can get your job done.

For both these groups of people, the following real-life examples demonstrate the pitfalls and consequences of proceeding without a clear plan. Throughout my career, I've had the opportunity to start new digital ventures within some of the largest multibillion-dollar companies in the world, as well as in tiny, self-funded startups with brilliant ideas. These businesses have been wildly different in nature, outlook, and behaviors, yet there was a common thread. By observing and studying the following examples, I realized that, while they are driven by different motives, the cost of failure for each of them would be equally devastating.

Kirsty's Story: Daring Entrepreneur Experiences Pitfalls First-Hand

Kirsty has been a professional acquaintance of mine for several years. She graduated from a top London university and worked for one of the Big Four accounting firms. She was a bright, high-flying, mid-level executive who was rising through the ranks. She was married to a professional and had everything going for her. Kirsty has always been an inquisitive go-getter and she believed she could make the world a better place. In her heart of hearts, she was an entrepreneur. The politics of a big firm became nauseating to her, so in her early 30s she did the unthinkable: she quit her job.

Prior to quitting, Kirsty had been involved in the London tech entrepreneurship scene and had seen how startups with the right idea, funding, and team can scale quickly. The plethora of startup incubators, seed funding, and the whole ecosystem and entrepreneurial lifestyle was appealing compared to the rat race. Kirsty figured her life savings of several hundred thousand pounds were enough to launch her novel idea, which could be London's new unicorn, joining the likes of TransferWise and Funding Circle.

Kirsty wanted to change the online, short-term rental market and how property owners listed their properties on various platforms such as Airbnb and Booking.com. She correctly identified that property owners were struggling to manage duplicate listings of the same properties across the various platforms. What if they could manage the listings on a single platform that automatically ensured they got the maximum rental from each one of those platforms?

From her experience, Kirsty knew the algorithms well and saw how her solution could earn much more for property owners while making their admin much simpler. Who wouldn't want this?

After doing all the right things—talking to numerous potential customers, understanding their pain points—Kirsty decided to build a prototype to show potential customers for feedback. She engaged an offshore software company based in the Ukraine to do this. Despite communication challenges with the software developers, Kirsty developed a prototype in 12 weeks and put it in front of her target customers. The feedback was encouraging, and the customers suggested several tweaks that would be useful for them. Kirsty was getting excited as her target audience was engaging.

She decided to go further and develop her prototype into a full-fledged solution. The estimated cost was a further £150,000 for a London-based software agency to build her software, which they did in six months. Kirsty was ready for the launch.

She took her new rental platform to market and saw instant success. However, along with this success came a challenge: customers started demanding further tweaks to meet their needs and this meant more software development. Kirsty had to decide whether she would spend more savings on these developments or raise the money to do it.

She decided to raise the funds. She quickly realized that venture capitalists avoid backing solo entrepreneurs, seeing them as too risky. Instead, they look for well-rounded teams consisting of tech, business, and operation experts with domain knowledge. Through networking at startup events, Kirsty linked up with her co-founders, who had the right tech and operational experience. She convinced them to join her unicorn hunt journey in exchange for nominal salaries and generous share options in the business.

The team energetically went to work to optimize the product and attract more paying customers. The tweaks they delivered attracted new customers, and revenues started coming in despite not being able to cover all operating costs. It was commonplace for the team to work 70-plus-hour weeks.

The new team soon ran into obstacles. Firstly, they were not aligned on how the product should be developed. Part of the team felt that their solution should stop at just listing properties on various platforms. Kirsty felt that, based on customer feedback, the platform should go deeper and provide basic accounting services to help manage the property owners' accounts. Simple experiments could have solved this contest, but then the real challenge started to emerge. The platform couldn't be easily or cheaply adapted to run these experiments without severely affecting existing users. The underlying technology developed by the London agency was created for a quick launch and not ongoing agility. Any ongoing experimentation of features would involve a near total rewrite of the platform. This put off the few investors who were willing to provide seed capital and keep the venture going.

Eventually, Kirsty's co-founders left, and she had to cease operations. She had lost most of her life savings and the whole episode nearly wrecked her marriage. However, as with all these things, she learned invaluable lessons and became wiser. Interestingly, she had numerous job offers from large organizations, who valued her corporate and startup experience.

Now Kirsty is back in an accounting job. In speaking with her, I sense that a thought lingers in the back of her mind: "Things could have been different."

She shared with me that her venture didn't get the vital funding at the right time for two reasons. Firstly, her team came across as disjointed at the crucial time in front of potential investors. Despite the force of her personality, there wasn't a common vision and goal unifying the rest of her team. However, the team would say they were simply 'being agile', but we will learn in this book that being agile successfully is so much more than simply acting quickly. Secondly, Kirsty wasn't a techie and didn't realize until it was too late that the technology the agency had created locked her in and slowed her down.

Both challenges are not difficult to solve. With the right knowledge and an end-to-end plan, Kirsty could have avoided both her challenges, more than likely raised funding, and got her business to scale.

While Kirsty's experience is a great example of the problems that show the need to build the right thing and inspire the agile digital strategy blueprint, these are as much inspired by the experiences of another associate of mine, Adam. I couldn't have written this book without him.

Adam's Story: The 'React and Transform' Corporate Dilemma

This case study comes from a large industrial conglomerate that owned several businesses, manufacturing and distributing a catalogue of over 500,000 products to small businesses in the building and construction space. This UK business has grown over time through acquisitions and has mainly sold its products through its 1,000-plus stores dotted around the country. Customers were generally loyal, and revenues grew steadily over the years until e-commerce players started disrupting the space. Through transparent price-based competition, these new digital entrants put pressure on the business's pricing model. Moreover, by offering nationwide deliveries on products ordered online, the new disruptors were rendering the bricks-and-mortar stores irrelevant.

The business was naturally deeply concerned and, based on the advice of some very expensive strategy consultants, the CEO believed a digital transformation was vital to save the business. The board accepted his story and sanctioned the necessary budgets. The newly appointed Chief Digital Officer then headhunted and hired Adam (not his real name) to deliver the digital transformation.

Within months of his arrival, Adam found himself a rising star within the business. Members of the executive openly declared their support for his digital transformation plan. Buoyed by this, Adam set about hiring a large team of technologists to implement his plans to introduce new digital services, such as a detailed online product catalogue, web-based customer services, and mobile apps.

Adam's trouble started when he reached the execution phase. As soon as he tried to deliver an online catalogue, he realized that the business stored product data in various silos to support its store operations. This was a showstopper but not new information. People who had been with the business knew of this situation but there was never a compelling reason to fix it until Adam's digital transformation kicked in.

The current product data setup was so vital to operations that it was decided that a separate Product Information Management (PIM) project was first required to sort out the data. Arguments over what data should be stored and who should manage it ensued. Given that the stores accounted for nearly 100% of the revenue and the online channel was merely a catalogue, commercial logic favored protecting the existing business. Consequently, the PIM project ended up delivering the needs of stores more than Adam's digital vision of having a single source of product truth for all channels (stores, web, mobile).

To add to Adam's frustrations, he was severely challenged in finding the right technology talent to execute his digital transformation plan. Digital architects, software developers, data management specialists, and digital marketers were all in short supply. Where were they? Seemingly not where the business was headquartered in the West Midlands, 130 kilometers north of London. Adam convinced the CEO, despite his reservations, that opening a technology development center in the heart of London was the solution. It was called the Technology Centre of Excellence and was set up with the requisite bright paints, pool tables, and minimalist furniture in an avant-garde tech hub in a regenerated warehouse district.

The center seemed to solve the tech talent problem, but soon cracks began to show. The 'old' IT team managing the company's legacy infrastructure and the 'new' team were on very different wavelengths and rarely saw eye to eye. Yet both relied on each other to deliver projects. Agile ways of working were introduced to the existing IT team and they were encouraged to start building solutions without too many requirements. The new team was encouraged to plan a little and have project plans so that the existing team could see what was happening and work accordingly. Needless to say, both teams were immensely frustrated.

After spending tens of millions on this digital transformation, the net results were a host of failed projects, a demoralized team, and increased costs. Very little in the way of benefits materialized. Adam lost his job and the CEO was dismissed by the board soon after. Ironically, Adam is still in high demand for the ever-growing digital transformation market, but the CEO has not been heard of since.

I knew Adam personally, since we studied for an MBA together. I caught up with him after his experience, now a much wiser man, and he smiled as he reflected insightfully on his experience:

> On reflection, digital transformation is a misnomer. It is almost impossible to transform an organization to something else. The bigger the organization, the more impossible it becomes. The reason is quite simple really. An organization grows over time to become successful. Its managers and executives are entrenched in certain values, beliefs, and behaviors, leading to success. When faced with the threat of a digital disruptor, their instinct is to react and change but there is a stronger instinct to protect what is there, be it existing sales, systems, people, or ways of doing things. Eventually, old ways win and die hard. Amidst all this, you have collateral damage, such as me and my CEO.

I've met many Adams. They are surprisingly common. The real tragedy is that all of this could have been avoided. A builder doesn't set about constructing a house without architect's drawings. An engineer doesn't build an aircraft without a plan. Yet every day, in countless organizations, executives and managers start reactive digital transformation initiatives without a clear understanding of the goal, customer benefits, or what is truly required to succeed. Had Adam's company looked at the whole transformation from a customer point of view, developed a clear goal, and adopted a truly agile mindset, they would have approached the problem differently.

It isn't just the millions in shareholder's money that is wasted, but human potential. Careers are wrecked, and psyches scarred for life. Yet all this is so avoidable. This reality is my main driver to help startups begin in the right way and for existing organizations to implement change in a considered way.

This book sets out to provide a simple way to have an end-to-end, customer-centered digital strategy. It highlights the right agile mindset, team, and technology to deliver it. In short, a plan to make visions a reality and avoid wrecking careers.

Adam and Kirsty: What Can We Learn?

There are too many Adams and Kirstys. Like many of their fellow entrepreneurs and corporate employees, they are looking to achieve certain things. While it is easy to mistake this drive for a pursuit of material success, deep inside they are merely trying to express themselves. Deep inside, we know that we can make a difference and want ourselves and others to experience the benefits of our hard work. There is real joy in that. Material success is a by-product. When that expression is stifled due to lack of clarity or the inability to convince others to see what we see, we despair and give up. That is the real waste.

However, we can tilt the odds of success in our favor with a clear plan and the ability to engage and energize others. This is what this book is about, and I hope you discover that magic through the tools I've provided here. Use them to bring to life your entrepreneurial idea, align a team behind you, and go after success.

Reflecting on my own career, applying this method has always helped me influence stakeholders and win the necessary resources required to launch initiatives. I cannot think of an instance where I initiated a project using this framework and didn't get the resources required to execute it. Hence, I know that this framework works in energizing those around you to take action. All I ask of you is that you approach the concepts explained in this book with an open mind. They can be applied rigorously to your own circumstances; since these ideas are universal by their nature, the advice offered in this book can be applied to businesses of any type.

How to Use This Book?

Now I would like to lay out the book's structure for you. Firstly, I've developed it in a way that follows the logical sequence in which people actually go about launching a successful venture. Secondly, the structure is such that, by going through each step in sequence, you will incrementally build the right knowledge and a clear plan. By the end of the book you will have a blueprint for success customized for your venture.

Here's a quick reminder of the agile digital strategy blueprint's five key areas from earlier:

1. Plan
   a. Where do you compete?
   b. How do you compete?

2. Execute
   c. Agile Mindset
   d. Agile Teams
   e. Agile Technology

Each section of the book explains a step in the blueprint formation and provides a simple visual to summarize it. You are strongly encouraged to think through and use each section's template before you move on. The accompanying website to this book at hajajdeen. com provides the templates that you can use to work on each framework section.

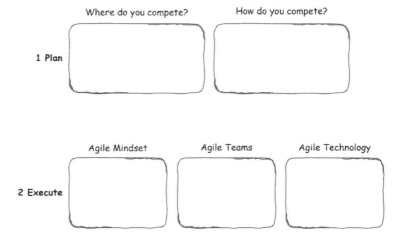

At the end of each section, I've included a resources section where I've curated a collection of relevant articles and online tools. I've carefully selected these to complement the content in this book, and each resource will be very useful in thinking through what you want to fill out in each template.

In the first phase of the agile digital strategy blueprint we will address planning, which involves two key questions from the above diagram. Any new venture, be it a startup on a shoestring or a new initiative within a multibillion-dollar business, needs to clearly answer:

a. Where is the venture competing?
b. How it is going to compete in that space?

The concepts and examples explained in the first phase will help you to answer these questions for your startup, business idea, or corporate initiative.

In the second phase of the blueprint, we will cover the execution, which is where you put your plan into action. The key consideration here is: what resources are required to execute your plan? The answer to this question will relate to three categories:

a. Agile Mindset
b. Agile Teams
c. Agile Technology

By exploring each of these areas in detail, you will gain an understanding of how they will form and drive your business.

Essential to the message of this book is the notion that any such venture you are likely to be launching will be agile by its nature. Agile, in this case, is the mindset and behaviors to solve customer problems and delight them quickly and continuously.

In addition, it is safe to assume that a digital philosophy will underpin your business, if in fact it isn't at the core of the business. Therefore, this book combines a strategic approach and executes it using an agile methodology.

Overall, the blueprint outlined in this book lies at the intersection of competitive strategy, digital, and agile mindset. By following this framework, you will be well on your way to success.

Why Plan?

It seems contradictory to plan while adopting an agile mindset. Should we not throw caution to the wind? Get started? Learn by doing?

I'm asked these questions all the time. Regardless of whether it is a startup or a corporate, these questions arise again and again.

The first question and area of confusion arises from what is being planned. Many involved believe the plan calls for a Gantt chart-type project schedule that clearly shows who does what and by when. Any self-respecting agile practitioner would frown upon such a plan. We all know projects don't get delivered according to Gantt charts for the simple reason that we are human. However, the cause of the confusion is that we are talking about an execution plan here and not a business strategy. The reason for this is conditioning. Hence, people involved in execution naturally think of plans as project plans.

Secondly, people who have read about or have earned some certification in 'agile' learn an approach in which you assemble a small, autonomous team of experts and get them started. This team will define what the product or venture looks like and determine when it will be delivered. The business strategy is planned within the head of the charismatic lead entrepreneur if it is a startup, or passed down from the board if it is a corporate setup. The real problem in both instances is the lack of ownership and engagement by the team that is actually running the show. When you perceive an idea as not being born in your head, you are not nearly as engaged as when you think it was your idea. Moreover, the deeper the analysis, the more engagement you see in teams, as they spark up when they discover an insight.

The planning we talk about in this book is the strategic business planning that answers the critical questions of where and how you are going to compete. Answers to these provide clarity, and clarity energizes the team. Conversely, confusion drains the team of vital energy. We have all seen this.

Winning teams are involved in strategy creation from the onset. This helps them to zone in on a niche and figure out how to serve customers in that micro-niche better than anyone else.

When teams discover where their niche is, half the plan is in hand, so it is here that we start.

The essence of strategy is choosing what not to do.

~ Michael Porter ~

PLAN

Chapter 1
Where Do You Compete?

From Clarity to Confidence

A few friends and I used to advise selected startups and small businesses on their business strategy. At the end of every startup pitch I used to ask the presenter four questions:

1. Which sector is your business in?
2. Which industry are you in?
3. Which niche are you targeting?
4. What are the profitable segments within your niche?

While the response was always confident, what I was really looking for was clarity. We rarely saw clarity. In the odd instance we did, and history tells us that the startup with clarity of purpose always goes on to succeed. The situation isn't too different when it comes to seasoned managers at large corporations. During my consulting experience I still saw a lot of confident presentations but not one backed by clarity.

However, if you are starting up a business it's vital that you have 100% clarity on the above questions for two good reasons. Firstly, the existence of an established sector and industries with many competing companies is good. This may seem counterintuitive, but it means there is strong customer demand for the products or services in that sector and industry. It also validates your venture idea, meaning that when it grows and is operating successfully, your business will be a competitor in this space.

All the US companies listed in the S&P 500 are grouped into 11 sectors. The total value of these companies was around US$50 trillion as of June 2019. The 11 sectors are further refined into 168 industries. The London Stock Exchange has a similar classification, as do other exchanges around the world.

The presence of valuable companies in the industry group means you are disrupting an existing market. There is proven revenue and profits to be had and the market is worth disrupting. You can be confident that yours is not an academic research venture for which there is no demand.

Secondly, your investors, backers, team, and you will one day want a lucrative exit. The strength of the market means that you can either sell into a competitor or list on the stock exchange within your industry classification.

In this chapter I will share with you my experience of reaching clarity on these basic questions. Giving them genuine consideration can lead to exciting new ideas within the sector of your choice. Remember the moments when you had that idea that will change the world, and the excitement that went with imagining your idea turn into the next Amazon, Uber, or Facebook. Then came the frustrating realization that if only the venture capitalists, bankers, employees, and customers understood what your business was all about, success was inevitable. It is a lot easier to convince others when you yourself are crystal clear. Clarity bestows confidence.

Where do you compete?

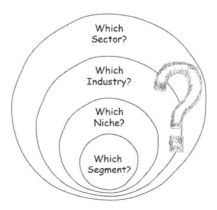

Let's work through this section of the blueprint and get to clarity.

Consider the above diagram, which you will fill out for your own venture, as layers of an onion. The aim is to get to the center, where we find absolute clarity, but first we must peel back all the layers and really understand the landscape in which the new business will operate. In the following sections we will delve into each layer.

Which Sector Are You In?

A sector is the top-level grouping. For example, consumer discretionary is a sector within the S&P 500 classification. As of June 2019, companies under this sector were worth US$5.3 trillion combined and had grown in value by 8% in the preceding 12 months. (Please see the Resources section at the end of this chapter to see all sector groupings and their respective financial performance.)

The sector, in my view, is merely a validation that the venture you are contemplating will satisfy a genuine mass need when operational. This stops you from conjuring up services for which there is no real demand.

It is when we look at the next layer, industries within a sector, that new venture possibilities start to emerge.

The Industry—Your Real Playground

When we drill down into a sector we get to its industries. Under these industries we have the individual companies providing the sector's products and services.

The US consumer discretionary sector we looked at has 11 industries. These are auto components; automobile; distributor; diversified consumer services; hotels, restaurants, and leisure; household durables; internet and direct marketing retail; leisure products; multiline retail; specialty retail; and textile, apparel, and luxury goods.

So, what industry did Uber disrupt? While we perceive Uber as having disrupted taxi companies, it actually has disrupted the transportation industry. It has redefined the customer experience through its ride-hailing app and changed the entire economics of the transportation industry in the consumers' favor. An Uber ride today in most cities is cheaper than the same taxi ride five years ago. This dramatic disruption of a large industry is what has fueled Uber's meteoric adoption and growth.

When low-cost budget airlines such as Air Asia and Ryanair entered the market, they started to disrupt inefficient and sometimes profitable national airlines. The significant reduction in ticket costs caused passengers to adopt low-cost airlines in droves, plunging many national airlines into bankruptcy.

Both Uber and low-cost airlines are interesting because they may appear to be the same sort of disruption, which ultimately lowered prices for customers, but they are not. This is where understanding the industry distribution helps define your profitable entry.

If we plotted all the companies against their profitability within the transportation industry, we would probably get a bell curve as shown below.

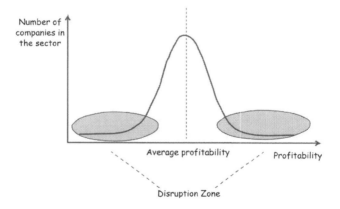

Most companies would be making average profits, we would have a group of companies with poor profits, and another group making above average profits. Taxi companies would have poor profits due to stiff competition and high costs. National airlines would have been highly profitable as they were near monopolies but squandered their profits due to inefficiencies.

In our analysis, Uber disrupted the low profitable taxi industry, whereas low-cost airlines disrupted the national airlines, which had hidden profits. Both were sleepy and complacent industries in my view. Taxi firms probably considered themselves immune to major disruption as they had little incentive to invest and improve customer experience. 'No one would disrupt our low profit space' must have been the prevailing wisdom. Then Uber arrived.

Bloated national airlines, on the other hand, must have relied on their monopolies. Then the low-cost airlines arrived.

When you are considering your own venture, which part of the industry are you disrupting?

Understanding the sector and industry helps you to see the macro picture, the 30,000 feet view. However, just having this view isn't enough. We now need to reveal the next layer, and it is here that we find profitable niches where new ventures can thrive.

Which Niche Are You Targeting?

In every industry there are hidden niches, which entrepreneurs have time and again exploited profitably. Why do these niches exist in the first place? If competition is as brutal as we think, customers in these niches would have been served by existing market players. As such, no new entrant could make a profitable entry, surely. The reason these niches exist is because as businesses grow, they are taught to focus on their largest and most profitable customer segments. This leaves behind groups of customers who are dissatisfied with what is on offer from existing companies. They tolerate these dissatisfactory offers until a better proposition comes up from a new player.

Harvard professor Clayton M. Christensen explains this well in his book *The Innovator's Dilemma*.

Industry Niche

Vente-privée (now rebranded as Veepee.com) is a French e-commerce company that pioneered the model of online flash sales. It sells designer brands exclusively to members, with prices discounted by 50%–70%. These sales include a diverse selection of product categories: fashion, accessories, toys, watches, home appliances, sports equipment, technology, and wines.

Veepee.com targets a specific niche of customers who are after discounted luxury goods with one-off novelty. They are the antithesis of Amazon, which sells everything to everybody. In 2015, Veepee.com had revenues of US$2.5 billion having only been operating for 14 years by then. This is an example of how, with a focused niche within a large industry, a new player can carve a profitable space all for themselves.

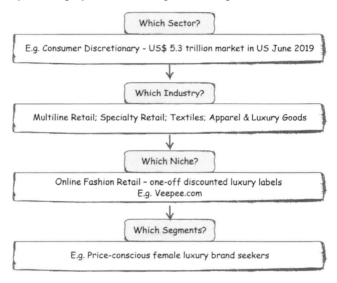

Value Chain

There is another method to find a profitable niche within an industry. While Veepee.com found its profitable niche by drilling deeper and deeper vertically from the top down, another way to look is horizontally across the industry's value chain.

What does the value chain in which your business operates look like? Who supplies and who consumes what at each stage? Is it end-customer facing (B2C) or are you a solution provider to an intermediary in the value chain (B2B)?

Let's say your new venture involves providing technology services to retail businesses. By looking across the retail distribution industry, you would first figure how the value chain is organized. Thereafter you can map the core technology that each of these players uses to serve their customers. This can be a revealing exercise.

By understanding the value chain, the underpinning technology, and current frictions, you can then start to position your solution.

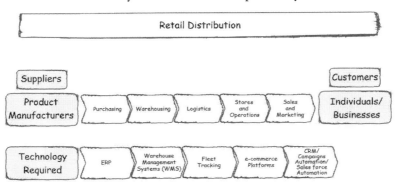

Having led numerous e-commerce teams, I'm relentlessly contacted by technology suppliers promising a cool technology that is supposed to delight customers and skyrocket our sales. We usually have little time for these speculative sales attempts as they fail to understand an important factor: teams are usually trying to fix a customer issue further upstream. Digital marketing teams, for example, could be pushing their e-commerce colleagues to improve on the delivery proposition, therefore reducing friction for the customers. The marketing teams then use this improvement as a point of differentiation and competitive advantage.

Understanding the impact of the problem you are solving helps you target the right buyers for your product and opens up new possibilities. This may not be evident easily but an analysis using a tool such as the above helps immensely.

If you are doing a deep dive here, this is where domain expertise can be invaluable. If you are an expert in the field you are disrupting, you should know the value chain, friction, and possible solutions intuitively. However, if your background is from a different industry, you can still be a disruptor, as long as you have surrounded yourself with knowledgeable people and experts in their field.

One way I've found useful, deep industry knowledge is by using platforms such as GLG and Guidepoint (see the Resources section). These services match industry experts with those seeking information. You can find numerous former executives of well-known organizations offering their insider knowledge through such platforms.

What Are the Profitable Segments Within Your Niche?

When you have reached clarity on your niche, you will have a clear idea of the group your product or service will target. It is always beneficial not to think of groups of people in the abstract but to understand them as individuals.

Before the digital age, most businesses operated locally. Owner-operated businesses especially had to form a deep understanding of their customer needs and motivations. Successful entrepreneurs made this into an art form. They intuitively grasped what their customers wanted and how their customer needs were changing over time. Sam Walton, who started with a single retail store, grew his business to the largest retail empire in the world, Walmart. During the time he grew Walmart, he did not have access to big data, analytics, cloud computing, or any of the other technologies now branded a business essential. He spoke to customers and employees, then acted decisively and quickly. He worked out that not all of his shoppers were the same, so he segmented them and tailored propositions accordingly.

So how do we reproduce the success that Sam Walton achieved?

Fortunately, we now have access to far more tools than we would ever need to separate customers into various segments. Mostly they are only theoretical; however, Google Keyword Planner is one tool that has repeatedly worked in my various ventures. It is a free tool provided by Google to help advertisers find out the number of searches on each keyword and elated keywords. This can be very useful to determine customer demand. By analyzing the related keywords and phrases that customers are searching for, we can identify different segments within your chosen niche and what the motivation is for those segments.

Understanding the segments that you are targeting, and their drivers, will become immensely useful in the execution phase, where you design a compelling service for your segments.

Timing Your Entry

Think back to my story about co-founding Fast-Foods.net in 1999, one of the world's first mobile commerce apps. Yes, we enabled pizza ordering on the mobile internet as early as 1999! Those of you who have worked on internet technologies for as long as I have would recall that the first mobile internet was delivered through a technology called WAP (Wireless Access Protocol). The first Nokia and Ericsson phones had 14.4Kbps download speeds and had a tiny grayscale screen.

I engineered a mobile app that would work on those two phones, allowing users to place an order for a pizza and pay for it through their phone as well. The application worked well, and we launched it as part of our online service. Technically the solution was way ahead of its time and this invention alone skyrocketed the valuation of my startup to more than US$50 million. I once had the CEOs of the two largest mobile operators in Singapore vying to speak to me about the service we had launched and wanting to see a demo. I only realized the significance of this event much later.

So why were customers not queuing to adopt the solution? In hindsight, the reasons are obvious: user-friendly smartphones, such as the ubiquitous iPhones of today, were non-existent, and the poor interface of the initial internet-enabled phones made the experience of ordering over the phone superior to the mobile internet version. So, at the time there wasn't a compelling enough reason to switch. Fast forward 15 years and food ordering apps are now commonplace. Uber Eats, Just Eat, and Food Panda are used countless times a day. Smartphones, their ubiquity, high-speed 4G mobile access, and proliferation of addictive apps such as WhatsApp and Facebook, have all contributed to adoption. Simply put, Fast-Foods.net was a solution way ahead of its time and the market wasn't ready for it.

This brings us to two key considerations for anyone launching a startup either on their own or within a large corporation. Firstly, are customers ready to adopt your digital service and, secondly, is your overall timing right?

The Trend Is Your Friend

Interestingly, I've come to discover that the answers to both of those questions come not from the industry you are entering but from adjacent industries.

Industries embrace digital at different speeds. As of 2018, over 60% of books and over 80% of all flight tickets were booked online. Just ten years prior, these figures were dramatically lower. The flip side of this is that when we as consumers have experienced buying books online, we want the same experience for other products and services. This then triggers digitization in other industries.

If we look at online flight ticket booking, it started out by offering online flight information. After the ability to book flight tickets online was well accepted, marketplaces followed (e.g. Skyscanner and Hipmunk), which presented various airlines and hotels, as consumers wanted a one-stop shopping experience. Such marketplaces have since exploded and customers can now feel overwhelmed by choice. Market competition drives such evolution and we are seeing this happen faster than ever before.

Hence, if you are considering launching an innovative solution in a particular industry, the clues may lie in what adjacent industries have already achieved. Interestingly, different countries adopt digital technologies at different speeds as well. The propagation of internet access, smartphones, and cost all drive internet adoption in each country. However, consumers have similar pain points and drivers across countries. In India, e-commerce boomed after 2015, whereas it had already matured in the UK by then. So, transplanting the e-commerce learnings from the UK to India can provide players in the latter with a competitive advantage.

Is there then an opportunity to adopt what customers have already adopted in another industry or country within yours? For example, if you trade fashion products online, is the next wave a Skyscanner-like tool that helps customers compare the best prices on the exact same branded fashion piece across multiple sites? Can you make trends from other industries your friend for your own innovation?

Timing Can Be Everything

When we launched Fast-Foods.Net, the solution fulfilled a customer need, but customers were not ready for it until several years later. Hence, timing your entry, especially if it is an innovative business model, is key. One may argue that a radical innovation such as the iPhone caught on like wildfire when customers didn't even know that they needed such a device. However, while customers didn't know that the solution was an iPhone, they were already experiencing pain points with incumbent devices, such as small screens, fiddly navigation, and slow browsing. Therefore, ensuring that demand exists, either overtly or latently, is key to determining whether it is the right time for your solution.

Bill Gross summarizes this well in his TED video and you can find a link in the Resources section at the end of this chapter.

You can map where your industry is compared to adjacent industries using a diagram as shown below. This can inspire ideas on what can happen in your own industry.

While it is important to clearly understand the exact sector, industry, niche, and segment your business is entering, this is no use if you don't produce something that customers want to pay for! In the next chapter, 'How Do You Compete?', I share all about how we identify and design a business to do exactly that.

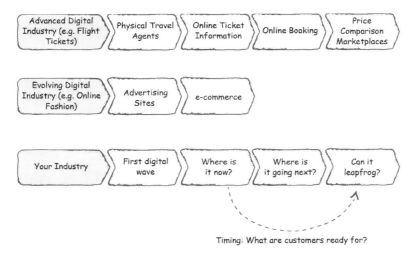

Timing: What are customers ready for?

Resources

Sector and Industry Information

You can find up-to-date data on the value of sectors and industry data on the Fidelity website. It shows the full list of the 11 sectors in the US, with their current value and historical financial performance. It also provides the financial performance of the 168 sub-industries.

https://eresearch.fidelity.com/eresearch/markets_sectors/sectors/sectors_in_market.jhtml

UK sector data based on stocks listed on the London Stock Exchange is available on shareprices.com. Companies are organized under 39 sectors. Individual companies are listed under these sectors.

https://shareprices.com/sectors

The United Nations Global Goals for sustainable development are a different way of deciding where you offer your solution. The 17 different goals set out to make the world a better place for all and not just the few. It is what the world needs, and if your solution delivers one of these goals, it may provide an added layer of meaning to you and your team.

https://www.globalgoals.org/

Mintel is a market research provider and has numerous pieces of research on niche industries, with deep insights and highlighting trends. It is a paid service and you can purchase individual reports. Some business libraries provide Mintel access.

https://www.mintel.com

If you are looking for deep industry expertise and would like to understand an industry by consulting with domain experts, GLG and Guidepoint are services that connect industry experts with those seeking industry insights. The experts are usually senior level executives or specialists who consult on a part-time basis. The engagements are governed by confidentiality so you cannot aim to get confidential information through them, but by asking the right questions you can uncover information not available in the public domain. Cost is based on the time spent with the expert and a fee for the platform.

https://glg.it/
https://www.guidepoint.com/

When it comes to understanding current actual demand for anything, there is no better source than Google if you know how to use its tools. Google Keyword Planner is a free tool that Google provides for you to see how many searches occur for a keyword, so that you can plan your advertising. It is an excellent proxy to gauge demand for anything by analyzing how many searches are being made for those keywords and related keywords you are interested in. After all, Google had over 87% of the search market as of June 2019. In addition, there are several posts and videos that describe how to find profitable niches using Google Keyword Planner.

Google Keyword Planner - https://ads.google.com/intl/en_uk/home/tools/keyword-planner/

Useful Book and Video

The Innovator's Dilemma by Harvard professor Clayton M. Christensen is a business classic that explains the power of disruption and why market leaders are often set up to fail. While it explains what incumbents can do to secure their market leadership, it is equally valuable for entrepreneurs to understand how to disrupt industries. The concept of targeting unloved customer segments in any industry is valuable for designing disruptive solutions.

Bill Gross's TED talk highlights the importance of timing in determining the success of new ventures. This point is often overlooked and can determine between wild success and dismal failure.

https://www.ted.com/talks/bill_gross_the_single_biggest_reason_why_startups_succeed?language=en

All men can see these tactics whereby I conquer, but what none can see is the strategy out of which victory is evolved.

~ Sun Tzu ~

Chapter 2
How Do You Compete?

So how do you compete? Many management thinkers, from Michael Porter to the authors of *Blue Ocean Strategy*, have provided various answers on how you compete. Having applied these models to digital strategy creation on many occasions, I believe there is a much simpler format when formulating digital strategy: combine elements of a competitive strategy but focus on the one person who matters most for your strategy to be successful—the customer.

Prior to the internet era, businesses could formulate a competitive strategy relative to their local competition by increasing their value to customers either through price, convenience, a wider range, or other service factors. However, there was little need to design a service that *delighted* customers. Things since then have changed with the proliferation of instant, transparent information, reviews, and ratings, as well as a vastly increased range of choice. This means that competitive advantage alone isn't enough. Businesses need to delight customers along their journey from start to finish and then be able to consistently repeat it. Businesses that have combined a digital-led, competitive strategy and designed a delightful customer journey now own entire markets.

In the period after the 2000 dot-com crash, several companies rose from the ashes to do just that and become digital giants. Amazon, eBay, Screwfix, and TransferWise are a few examples of companies that have used technology to create not just a competitive and differentiated offer but one that provides a delightful customer experience from start to finish.

So why does this approach work? It is easier to understand this when we flip the idea on its head and look it from the customer point of view. We as customers are on a mission to accomplish something. We then undertake a journey to fulfil that mission. Technology has made accomplishing the mission cheaper, faster, and more convenient than ever before but truly successful organizations have made the customer's journey to fulfil their mission a delightful one.

Would you try out a new service or product if you had no reason to do so? Unlikely. It is only when you perceive that the offering solves a problem or fulfils a desire, that you will be inclined to try it. In fact, you would be more likely to try it if you have been using a similar, dissatisfactory service and have been consciously or subconsciously looking for a better alternative. We all do this naturally. Then when the likes of an innovation such as Amazon or Apple's iPhone is launched, we take to them like fish to water.

Think of all the novel services or products you have tried but never returned to. The reason you didn't become a long-term fan of that short-lived novelty is because your experience wasn't delightful. You were not wowed! Had you been delighted, you would have become a repeat buyer and spread the word. As customers, we rave about experiences that delight us and cannot help recommending the product or service. This makes ideas go viral and it isn't a new phenomenon. The media through which ideas go viral has changed to Facebook, Twitter, and YouTube, but the underlying driver has not.

Fortunately, there is a step-by-step process to answering the key question of 'How do you compete?' which consists of the five steps shown in the diagram below.

How do you compete?

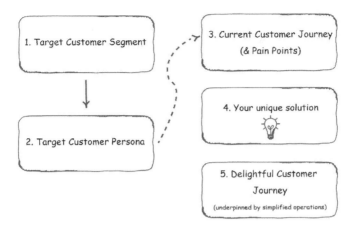

1. The first step is to understand your target customer segment. Who is it you are trying to serve?
2. The second step is to make the customer real. What is the profile of your ideal customer and what do they do from waking up to going to bed?
3. Thirdly and vitally, what are your customer's current journeys, especially their pain points along those journeys?
4. Next, how does your product or service fulfil your target customer's needs better than the existing competition?
5. Finally, you will create your ideal customer journey, which will delight your target customers, while making clear to them the factors on which your offer is superior to the competition.

Reach clarity on the above and you have a got a winning digital strategy on your hands. Go on to execute better, faster, and more cost-effectively than the competition and you have a winning business on your hands.

But before we dive deeper into serving your customer, do you know who they are?

Target Customer Segment

The first step is to understand the customer segment you will target. One proven way for startups to target a customer segment is low-end disruption.

Understanding how the various segments of customers are organized in your target industry helps you to prevent making the fatal mistake of trying to create products or services for markets that don't exist. A good example of doing this well was iPads, which were a solution to heavy laptops. Users didn't know they needed an iPad, but they knew the problems they faced with heavy laptops, so the market existed.

Low-End Disruption

If you are a startup or a new business within an existing corporation trying to capture a segment within an industry you need to start by targeting the unloved segments in your target market. There is sound economic rationale and evidence for doing this.

Clayton Christensen from Harvard Business School argues in his book, *The Innovator's Dilemma*, that tech disruptors are more successful in targeting the underserved customers within established industries.

By creating a solution for the frustrated customer within an existing industry, your product or service is likely to be a pain killer rather than vitamin, and what better than having an audience already waiting for your product. This may sound too good to be true but in every industry, as businesses grow, they leave behind a segment of customers who are not profitable to serve relative to their larger customers. Moreover, for incumbent businesses, serving these customers wouldn't make a meaningful addition to their existing revenues. Hence, they ignore any disruption in this space until it is too late for them to respond.

This strategy of targeting underserved customer segments has many benefits. It is likely to deliver to your business early adopters who are already experiencing the problems your solution solves. Secondly, the incumbents will ignore you in the early stages and not devote their considerable resources to crushing you, thus giving you the space and time to succeed. Thirdly, the smaller customers whom you delight today will more than likely be the larger customers of tomorrow. Your business will grow with them.

Screwfix: Low-End Disruptor to Market Leader

The building materials distribution industry in the UK has been disrupted in exactly this way. It is estimated to generate around US$15 billion in revenue per annum (at the time of writing in June 2019), primarily from supplying building materials to the trade and DIY enthusiasts. Prior to e-commerce, most building materials and tools were bought from local builders' merchants, whose most profitable customer segments were tradesmen, builders, and large construction companies. The DIY enthusiasts or retail customers represented only a small fraction of the merchants' revenue, so were not considered a high priority. However, the DIY enthusiast could buy large quantities of building materials if the merchants were willing to help the enthusiast with product knowledge.

This was a textbook opportunity for a disruptor. Enter Screwfix.

In 1999, Screwfix, a small hardware supplier based in Somerset, England, launched its website. Today it is one of the largest multichannel retailers in the UK with over US$1.4 billion in revenues. It attracts over ten million unique visitors to its website every month and customers can order from over 25,000 products.

From the onset, Screwfix focused on two segments: the DIY enthusiast and the 'white van tradesmen' who did ad hoc, odd jobs for households. The category of products that Screwfix brought to market, small tools and fixings, were not the core revenue generator of the builders' merchants, which generated most of their revenue through selling bricks, timber, and heavy building materials. Here was a perfect opportunity for Screwfix to disrupt at both the customer segment and product category levels.

Since their disruptive entry into the industry, Screwfix has scaled up to serve larger customers and taken the builders' merchants' lunch, who have collectively lost significant market share in the product category that Screwfix now specializes in. Screwfix has also expanded into plumbing and electrical products.

Economically and historically, entering with a laser-like focus to serve a niche, unloved segment within an established industry has proved wildly successful for new entrants who have executed the strategy well. It maximizes the chances of the startup attracting its first customers, refining its product, raising funds, and scaling up, all while incumbents are blissfully ignorant of their impending demise.

So, who are the underserved customers in the industry you are targeting? What does a Screwfix-esque solution look like for them?

Identifying your target segment is a useful exercise in two ways. Firstly, it validates whether there is a meaningful audience for your intended product. Secondly, it helps you build a persona of the actual customers you will build a product or solution for—not an imagined customer, but an actual potential customer with whom you can validate your minimum viable product.

Target Customer Persona

While the target customer segment analysis helps us understand both the existence of a viable customer as well as their aggregate needs, it is an intermediate step. It is an average. On its own it isn't useful to understand deeply the customers' needs and drivers. To do that we will need to focus on one individual customer.

Developing a Customer Persona

Any venture is trying to create a useful service for a group of people who value it sufficiently to pay for the service to keep the venture going. As such, a deep understanding of the motives and drivers of the group you are trying to serve is a vital first step. In this section we explore how to systematically understand and develop the customer persona of the target you are trying to serve.

One of my long-term goals has been to be involved in a property startup that made property investments super simple. The reasons were quite personal. Growing up in Singapore, I experienced first-hand how property ownership catapulted families into wealth and created a highly educated, affluent society. Over 90% of Singaporeans own their homes through a government housing program. As Singapore's economy grew, most of the population benefited from the increasing values of their homes. The small group that didn't own property was left behind.

When I moved to the UK the situation was different. While property was still a valuable asset in the long run that created financial independence and wealth, the number of people able to access property ownership was much lower. As of 2018, only 63% of the UK population owned their own homes. Yet, in the same year, the 4% of the population that are landlords owned over £1 trillion worth of properties, which were rented out to the 37% of the population that didn't own their homes. Hence, the rental market was mostly in the hands of a relatively small group of people.

I started to imagine a digital solution where property investments could be done easily with small amounts and diversified over several properties. The emergence of the crowdfunding phenomenon around 2014 caught my attention and I could see how it might be applied to property investments.

In 2016 I met the founders of Homegrown (www.homegrown. co.uk), two finance professionals from London with experience in the Big Four firms, who had the same idea and had built a property crowdfunding platform. Through Homegrown, savers can now lend directly to property developers through a regulated crowdfunding platform and invest from just £500 per property. It was easy to understand why this would be a winning model.

Then I did what most people would consider insane. I left a high-paying job as the Digital Transformation Director of a multibillion-pound turnover organization to join this yet unknown, unfunded startup, Homegrown. In my role as co-founder and Chief Technology

Officer of Homegrown, I set about applying over 20 years' experience in building and delivering web software, but this time without the corporate bureaucracy, PowerPoint, or politics.

The agile digital strategy blueprint I share with you in this book was developed in my mind and used over many years in the companies I worked with, such as Toyota, Saint-Gobain, IDA Singapore, and during the course of my MBA. However, it was at Homegrown where it was fully refined and truly tested in a startup.

As we learn how to build a customer persona, understand their *current* journey, and map their *ideal* journey, I will use my experiences at Homegrown to illustrate.

If you recall, in the previous chapter, 'Where Do You Compete?', we narrowed down to the micro niche that you are going to focus on. Having defined your micro niche, you can imagine a typical customer. When I say imagine, I'm not asking you to make them up. Rather, based on your first-hand interaction with those customers or through rigorous research, you should really understand these targets to a deep level.

When we raised first-round funding for Homegrown, a successful venture capitalist let us in on his criteria for selecting ventures to fund. He looks for founding teams with 'domain secrets', i.e. deep experience in the industry in which the venture is being founded, where the team has had first-hand interaction with customers in that industry.

If you already have the 'domain secrets' you should be able to understand and list the drivers and behaviors of your target customers. If you don't, the next best thing is if you have been a customer in that industry and have a list of improvements that your existing supplier can make. In this circumstance use yourself to write the persona.

If you have neither the domain secrets nor a user of the service you aspire to create, I strongly urge you to reconsider whether the micro niche you intend to target is the right one for you. I'm not suggesting that you cannot break into new industries and niches, but the odds will be stacked against you and you may struggle to raise finance, attract customers, partners, and income. Rather, reflect on your own history and find your unique perspectives in the industries you have been involved in. You will tilt the odds significantly in your favor.

Avoid mixing up a target customer persona and a marketing persona. In the target customer persona, we are looking at their:

- Basic profile
- Demographics
- Drivers and motivation
- Fears and challenges

Many proponents of customer persona definition inadvertently overlay the above information with additional data required for the marketing persona definition. Information such as the social media channels the target uses, how they consume information, and detailed analysis of their work are required at a later stage, when we are getting the word out.

When we developed the target customer persona for Homegrown, our profile looked like this:

Basic Profile:	Profile Photo	Drivers / Motivation / Goals:
Middle-aged professional with disposable income interested in investing through properties.		▪ Invest in property to get a better return compared to savings ▪ Prefers property investments over other asset classes
Demographics:		**Fears and Challenges:**
▪ Age: 35 ▪ Male ▪ Income: £70,000 p.a. ▪ Education: Basic Degree / Masters ▪ Location: London		▪ Investments not performing ▪ Losing out to peers ▪ Inflation eroding savings ▪ Insufficient time to source, check, and invest in individual properties ▪ Insufficient deposit to buy London properties ▪ High transaction costs to buy individual properties

Customer Persona Development Tips

1. When you launch your product to your initial target persona, don't be surprised that you attract other personas, or even if your initial adopters are different to the persona you created. Try to learn from those early adopters about how your product is serving them.
2. Use data as quickly as possible. Soon after you have launched your beta or product to market, use analytics tools such as Google Analytics to understand who is engaging with your product and who is not.
3. Avoid designing for non-existent personas based on averages. Validate first that the customers you are problem-solving for exist and the problem you are solving is real for them. Speak to these customers. They will tell you.

Once we have created the target customer persona it becomes easier to understand their current customer journey.

Current Customer Journey (and Pain Points)

Journey mapping is a holistic approach to understanding the flow of experiences a customer has when interacting with your business; it uses pictures and links to present the process graphically.

The objective of customer journey mapping is to create a visually expressed, deep understanding of the customers' experiences while they are traversing the path taken between having a need and getting that need met. Its intent is to 'get inside the customer's head' to understand the customer's experiences. The output of the customer journey mapping exercise can be fascinating.

Firstly, it will confer a level of clarity to you on what your target customer is trying to achieve and how that need can be met. Secondly, the clarity will bestow confidence for you to communicate your project and attract capital and talent to make it happen. It helps to sell your vision and catalyze people around it.

Putting a Customer Journey Map Together

Even if you have never mapped a customer journey, don't worry. The process is simple, and in this section I explain step by step the process that I use.

In the current journey we don't add any improvements that the innovation will bring to the customer, we just document the current real journey-pain points, warts, and all.

The future ideal journey contains all the innovations you plan to bring to your customers. At this stage don't worry if or how your solution will actually be delivered. We solve that later. Just free your imagination and create the most ideal journey for your customer; a journey that would delight them and make them your biggest advocate once they have experienced your product.

I've seen many entrepreneurs and intrapreneurs create just the new journey. While it may appear to be a shortcut, there are two key benefits in doing both the current and ideal journeys. Anyone you are sharing the idea with can immediately see the benefit of going with your solution versus the status quo. It demonstrates that you deeply understand the customer you are trying to serve and gives you and your idea credibility. It also shows that you are solving a real problem and not dreaming up a solution that then looks for a problem to solve.

In addition, by presenting both, you allow others to add to your ideas or reshape them. This can be powerful. When you have created that opening for your ideas to be refined by others, not only can it improve, but those stakeholders will become your supporters, as they are now vested in your progress. This can be immensely powerful in attracting teammates, capital, and partners.

Ian Merricks is the founder of the Accelerator Academy based in London. Ian has been a venture capitalist, and through his accelerator has helped hundreds of aspiring entrepreneurs to refine their startup idea, raise capital, and launch their businesses. One day, as I was standing with Ian on a London Underground platform awaiting the train, I took the opportunity to ask him, "What is your number-one criterion in choosing to work with a startup?"

In a considered and convincing fashion, Ian replied, "How teachable the lead entrepreneur is!" He was less concerned about the idea, market potential, and a superstar team, and more interested in whether the entrepreneur was a 'know it all' who had a monopoly over all good things that happen on earth. This entrepreneur is unlikely to engage or empower their team, financiers, and partners. I've seen too many examples of someone with a brilliant academic background, followed by a successful corporate career, perform dismally as an entrepreneurial leader.

By presenting your current and ideal journeys you demonstrate that you are willing to refine your ideas, are teachable, and are inviting others to participate.

Putting together your customer journey involves four steps:

1. Key Stages (in the customer's journey)
2. Thoughts
3. Customer Actions
4. Emotions

A blank customer journey map can look like the diagram below. There are digital tools to map the customer journey, and in the Resources section at the end of the chapter you can find links to some customer journey mapping tools.

Key stages define the major steps in a customer's journey. Below key stages we have different 'lanes' to capture thoughts, actions, and emotions.

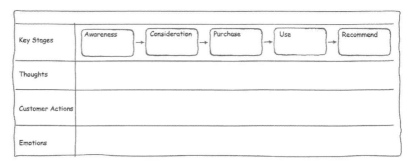

Key Stages

What are the key stages your customer goes through to get what they need? In most purchases it involves four main stages as outlined below. The stages may have different names depending on the type and size of purchase. What is known as comparison in a B2C scenario could well be a full-fledged tender in a B2B situation. However, most journeys would fit into the framework below.

1. Awareness
2. Consideration
3. Purchase
4. Usage

Awareness is when the potential buyer has identified a need and has a broad range of solutions to fulfil it. It isn't awareness in the marketing sense, where your solution is one of the choices available to the consumer, rather it is best to look at it from the customer point of view and get to what is driving the behavior.

Consideration is when awareness of a need is translated into a tangible range of possible solutions that can fulfil that need. At this stage, customers are mentally considering the various options available to them and what those options mean in terms of cost, effort, and reward. They may not be fully aware of the true costs and benefits of each of the potential solutions, but mentally start to frame those options. Clearly the effort and time spent on this exercise depends on the significance of the purchase. Is it a small purchase relative to income, or a large expense or investment? This drives whether customers spend a few minutes on deciding or consult a detailed comparison site and spend hours researching and comparing all options. They also tend to weigh up the risks of a poor choice. While it may not seem so, most customers at least do this subconsciously for a purchase of any significance.

Customers now have more information at their disposal than ever before when considering any purchase decision. From product information, comparison websites, user reviews and ratings, to social media chats, customers now have access to free and transparent information like never before.

Once satisfied that they have compared sufficiently, customers then decide on a choice and part with their cash to **purchase** the product.

The next step is when they **use** the product or service they have just purchased and experience it. This is the most important step from the customer's point of view. Thinking through in detail exactly how your product is consumed is key to completing the customer journey. While you as the provider would be unlikely to be interacting with the customer when they are consuming your product, you should be accessible through customer service touchpoints. If the customer needs help, these are opportunities to create a delightful experience when it matters most. How will your customer consume your product? What would delight them and make them share their positive experience?

You will notice that the customer journey maps a fifth stage called 'Recommend'. This is a vital factor for your new product to get 'word of mouth' referrals. The majority of new services don't get recommended. The few that succeed in this critical stage do two things very well. Firstly, their products are designed to delight customers. Secondly, they make it easy for their customers to spread the word. To do this while understanding the customer's thought process is key.

Thoughts

As customers go through each key stage in the journey they inevitably have thoughts. Whether they are stating observations to themselves as they go or are mentally asking questions, they are going through some thoughts. It is important that we capture these if we are mapping out the customer journey. One of the best ways to do this is to talk to potential customers and ask the right questions. Understanding the various thoughts that a person has during the customer journey is vital to understanding functional needs. If your product doesn't meet their functional needs, your customer won't consider your product or service as fit for purpose and you won't make the sale.

Some simple but highly effective questions you can ask to uncover customers' thoughts are:
- What is bothering you when you do this step in your journey?
- What are you thinking when you are doing this?
- What comes to mind when you are doing this step in the journey?

- What do you think others are thinking when they are doing this step?

Actions

As part of the customer's journey, they will take actions to move them closer to the end of the journey. This could be researching their desired product online, visiting or calling a local retailer, reading reviews, or preparing the funds to make the purchase. On the surface it isn't possible to uncover all of these actions unless you speak with your target customers (or know them deeply) and ask the right questions. You will be surprised how many of these actions in the journey are unexpected or perhaps even unnecessary. Some questions that will help you uncover these actions are:
- What are you trying to achieve here?
- What is the key outcome you desire?
- What did you do before?
- What did you do after?
- Were your actions face to face, through phone, email, or a website?

A customer will encounter different touchpoints during their journey. All of these should be captured under the 'Customer Actions' lane.

Emotions

Apart from various thoughts, the potential customer is experiencing emotions as they go through the key stages of the journey. They could be overwhelmed with the choice, confused by the details of each offering and how they can compare, outraged by a certain price, curious about a product review, and so on. To me the customer's emotions matter more than thoughts. Your product needs to be functionally fit to be considered a viable choice. However, if you delight the customer emotionally you can stand apart from the competition and own your space.

Some key questions here are:

- What are you feeling when you do this step?
- What would delight you in this step?

Daniel Priestley in his book, *Oversubscribed,* explains with compelling examples that consumers make emotional decisions when purchasing. It is easy to understand why. Often the purchase itself is made to fulfil an emotional need.

Customer Journey Mapping Tips

1. Our objective with the journey mapping is to create a sufficiently detailed appreciation of the customer's journey so that we can create a better version powered by our new solution. Hence, it is useful to keep the entire journey in mind and map end to end, as our objective here is to create a winning digital strategy, so the overall journey is what we are after.
2. The template provided will help you get started. However, if you would like to map a complex journey, I recommend the digital tools mentioned in the Resources section at the end of this chapter, which I've found useful. They have their own strengths and are suited for different situations.
3. While mapping, keep your focus on the target customer persona you are working with. If in the mapping process you discover a new persona, make a note, and keep this aside. If required, you can do an additional map for the new persona.
4. When you are doing this as a team, ensure someone is nominated and has the authority to rein the team back into working on the agreed persona as well as the entire journey.

Your Unique Solution

By now you should have clarity on your target customer persona, their current customer journey, and the ideal journey your new product will provide. This is a good start but not enough to create your winning digital strategy. We need to understand your competition and, importantly, engineer your new solution to be superior from the customer's point of view. This is key and is the reason this book exists. When you engineer a superior service, you get a chance at traction. Make that value fit fully in line with the customer journey and you have significantly increased the chances that your new product will get the traction it needs to become a thriving venture.

We will engineer your new solution using a three-step process.

Make Your Unique Value to Your Customers Stand Out

Every industry competes on several factors, such as price, convenience, and superior customer service. These factors have evolved over a long time, and industry insiders subconsciously compete on these factors. Disruptive new entrants tend to change the factors on which competition takes place and rewrite the rules of the game. If successful, they attract such a mass customer base that they permanently reshape the industry and often the incumbents cannot respond, and they fail spectacularly. Think what Amazon did to bookstores.

The common factors of competition are:
- Better price
- Save time
- Simpler to use
- More convenient
- Is fun
- Enhances image
- Reduces risk

Beneath these main factors are subfactors of competition. These are unique to your industry and the target customer. In Homegrown's case, to the customer 'saves time' means less time spent on property searches, viewings, mortgage applications, and tenant management.

To fully appreciate the factors of competition, you can list the main and subfactors for your product and consider them against two of your closest competitors. Often, entrepreneurs believe they don't really have direct competitors. This is a danger sign. If your product is an innovation and isn't used by customers now, then do they really need it? Commercially successful ventures often provide what customers already want in a better, faster, cheaper manner. Consider:

- What are customers' alternatives if they don't use your product?
- How do they do it now?
- Are there simpler ways to achieve the customers' end goals without using your product?

Choose your competitors the same way your customers would choose them. The customer's alternative to your solution is a well-understood existing solution. Always see the solutions from the customer's point of view and what value they derive from the solution. By making a customer value map you can spot what your competition offers now and the gaps that your new product can fill.

I recommend that you download the template hajajdeen.com to fill out the customer value map table. The purpose here is to check if indeed you have a differentiated offer relative to your competition. If it isn't clear to you, then you can be sure your customer won't understand it.

Competition Factor	Competition Subfactors	Close Competitor 1	Close Competitor 2	Your Product
Better Price	E.g. Subfactor 1 Subfactor 2	Describe how the competition does on this factor		
Saves Time				
Simple to Use				
More Convenient				
Is Fun				
Enhances Image				
Reduces Risk				

Ensure Your New Solution Radically Alters the Proposition

Now that you have the first draft of the customer value map, we can refine it. It is through this refinement that you start to sharpen your business model to be more competitive. To achieve this let's use the ERIC process. The ERIC process, in various guises, is taught in most top business schools as part of their strategy course. ERIC is an acronym for Eliminate, Reduce, Increase, Create.

As we begin to understand each of these in detail, keep your first draft customer value map in mind and reflect on how your offer can be refined using these tools.

Eliminate

What are the competitive factors entrenched in the industry that the current customer doesn't value highly? In other words, if these factors were eliminated, the customer wouldn't mind and would perhaps even be delighted. Amazon first eliminated the need to go into a bookstore to buy a book by delivering the same book to your doorstep. Consumers loved it because now they didn't have to make a trip and they still got the book. Then Amazon eliminated the paper book itself by delivering the digital version to you through Kindle. Readers adopted Kindle because they got the information they wanted without paper books gathering dust around the house.

Elimination is important, not just to enhance the customer journey, but it also reduces your operating costs. By eliminating physical bookstores Amazon avoided rental, labor, and various other associated costs, which means a saving can then be passed onto consumers. Through Kindle digital format Amazon eliminated printing and physical distribution costs. Kindle versions of the same book can be priced lower and reach a wider audience. While you are engineering your business model, elimination helps you to cut costs and to simplify.

One way to look at elimination effectively is to get into the mind of the customer and ask what their end goal is. What is it they are really trying to achieve? They are not trying to buy a book, but to get knowledge. If you approach it from that perspective, eliminating certain factors will help you provide a simpler, leaner service to your customers. It also helps you to innovate in a way that helps your customers achieve their end goals in ways they didn't anticipate.

If you recall the low-end disruption we touched on earlier, your competition's offer is an overkill for your target customer persona. These customers are not looking for the bells and whistles that other suppliers provide with inflated costs, rather they are looking for the simpler, lean service at a low price.

A lean business model isn't just simpler for the customer and more cost-effective, but as the business scales up, the number of people required to operate the business will be fewer and you can scale up with just a small team.

So, what can you eliminate from your first draft of the customer value map?

Reduce

After eliminating the unnecessary factors, you can focus on other factors that can be reduced without affecting the customer in a negative way. These are usually nice-to-have features from the customer perspective. Customers will compromise on these features if they are convinced that they are getting superior benefits.

When Henry Ford launched his first car, the Model T, he told customers they could have any color as long as it was black, yet the Model T sold phenomenally because color was a nice-to-have factor from the customer point of view. This approach is now being replicated by Tesla, which has only two models in production. By focusing on the electric car benefits, Tesla can get away with offering limited model choice. This approach is lean because it reduces operational complexity in production.

As a startup, the goal here is volume not variety. Variety creates exponential production and operational complexity, and higher costs. If you reduce the nice-to-have options, this increases your chances of getting to deliver sufficient volumes of your product to reach profitability.

Running out of cash is a top reason why promising startups shut down. If you can get to profitability as soon as possible, you have the luxury of waiting for further growth.

What features from your product can you reduce relative to current offers?

Increase

After you have eliminated and reduced certain factors, you can now move on to the more innovative part of the process where you innovate and increase the value to the customer. These are the factors that you want to compete on by increasing significantly above your competition.

The advantage of improving on an existing factor is that the customer is already familiar with the concept. As such, they already have a mental anchor to compare your new improved version against. The benefit of this familiarity cannot be underestimated. Unlike a totally new concept, which requires explanation, improving on an existing factor is easier to communicate and for the audience to absorb.

Create

Most digital startups also create new features within their product. These new features are meant to enhance the overall customer experience or deliver the service in the first place. The recent boom in peer-to-peer lending within the financial technology space has allowed savers to lend directly to borrowers cutting out many middlemen. Companies such as Funding Circle have grown tremendously and lend over £1 billion a year as of 2019. By creating a digital peer-to-peer platform, Funding Circle matched borrowers directly with savers who sought better returns on their savings. This has radically altered the industry.

As such, it is important to understand that what you are creating may be an underpinning factor, in this case a digital platform, to deliver the benefit, higher returns on savings, which is valued by your customer, and the customer themselves may be less interested in your novel creation.

Once you have gone through this ERIC process, you can summarize your radically improved proposition using the table below. This template is available to download from hajajdeen.com.

Eliminate	Reduce	Increase	Create
Factor 1	Factor 5	Factor 7	Factor 9
Factor 2	Factor 6	Factor 8	Factor 10
Factor 3			
Factor 4			

To see the ERIC process in action, let's revisit Homegrown. In Homegrown's case, the customer's close alternatives are either investing directly in a property or through a Real Estate Investment Trust (REIT), which are traded like stocks on stock exchanges.

Homegrown's property crowdfunding customer value proposition is significantly different from that provided by the alternatives. Compared to directly investing in property, Homegrown's proposition saves significant time, hassle, and fees, and is much more convenient overall in achieving the same goal. It is much more like investing through a REIT but provides the added benefit of more transparency and control, as you can now link investments directly to a property, unlike a REIT.

Homegrown's new proposition can be summarized as:

Eliminate	Reduce	Increase	Create
Property search Financing search	Risk (through smaller investments)	Speed to invest	Digital transaction system
Property ownership		Transparency	Regulated process
Transaction costs		Diversification	
Ownership hassle			

Ensure Your New Proposition Fits Well with the New Ideal Customer Journey

It is evident that Homegrown used all parts of the ERIC process to create a radically different proposition. However, the customer wouldn't understand this unless this new proposition worked to convert the customer's old journey into a delightful new journey. It is when we overlay the ERIC process on top of the new customer journey that the magic happens and we get to a new journey, which delivers the mission far better than the old way.

The most important part of your new solution design is ensuring that the value proposition you have created with the customer value map and ERIC process works with the different stages, and is overlaid on the current customer journey to derive the new customer journey. Below is a template that shows you how to overlay your new value proposition on the current customer journey.

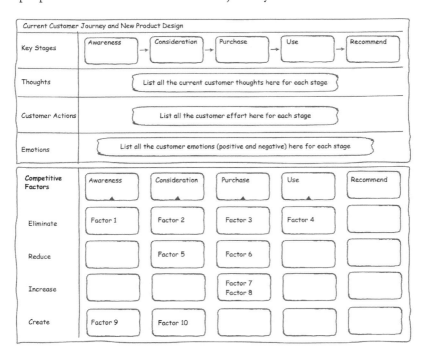

In the final step, when you create your new journey, the customer who undergoes this new journey should find the whole process far better than what they were used to. They should be delighted. They should notice all the pain points you have eliminated or reduced, and notice the aspects that have improved.

There is a good reason for this. Humans always relate a new experience to ones they have had before. They need an anchor point to compare. This is how our brains work.

When Nokia released the first internet-enabled phones, there was little adoption. Users were aware of these devices but using the internet was fiddly on these small devices. The iPhone changed everything. When it was released, the internet experience was far superior to the existing phones and not far from the experience of browsing the internet on PCs. Users were hooked. Let's see this process in action using the Homegrown journey.

Homegrown Customer Journey

Homegrown has made property investments faster, easier, more accessible, and created a host of other benefits. This becomes more apparent when you consider what the 'old' customer journey was for someone investing in property. It was a process filled with anxiety and uncertainty for most. Typically, an investor would save up the deposit required for the property investment, research the area and property, do viewings, make offers, apply for a mortgage, take possession of the property, find a suitable tenant, rent it out, then wait patiently for the investment to appreciate. While I make this sound simple, it isn't. The mere hassle of the whole process puts many off and prevents them from benefiting from long-term economic growth and achieving financial freedom.

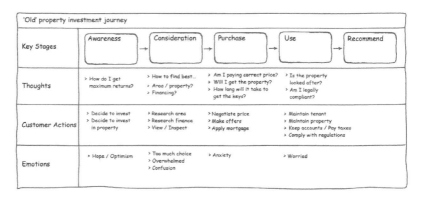

If you have spoken with anyone who has gone through the 'old' property investment journey they will tell you it is filled with anxiety, and if you are new to the game you will make costly mistakes. We believed that the whole process could be done online, made much easier, and as a result help those who wanted to invest in properties but simply didn't have the deposits, knowledge, and time to get property investment right. This we believed would help more individuals invest directly into property development projects and help developers build more homes.

Having understood our target customer persona, their drivers, and their current journey, we were able to conceive the new ideal online journey we wanted to deliver.

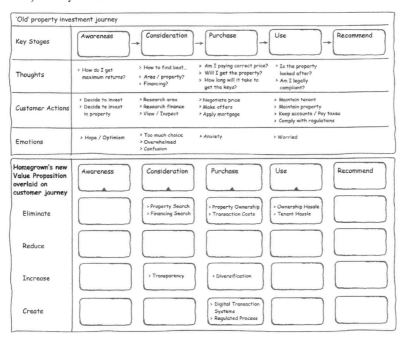

Now anyone wishing to invest in property simply needs to register on the Homegrown website, invest, and monitor. It is mind-boggling how simplified the new journey is compared to the traditional property investment journey. The new simplified process can be explained to potential customers using a simple diagram as shown below. When we demonstrated the new approach of property crowdfunding through an online platform to seasoned property investors, inevitably they had a broad smile and said, "This is the future of property investing."

The simplicity of the new online property crowdfunding model is achieved by keeping the customer journey simple, while taking much of the administrative hassle out of the user's hands. This is summarized by the new journey.

1. REGISTER
Sing-up and complete the registration process free of charge

2. INVEST
Choose a property and invest from £500 upwords

3. MONITOR
Monitor the performance of your portfolio through your dashboard

Ideal Customer Journey (Underpinned by Simplified Operations)

The solution we worked through with Homegrown as an example shows the new customer journey underpinned by a radically new business proposition. It is important to note that the new business proposition is not only simpler and cheaper for the customer, but it is also operationally simpler and cheaper for the business. Otherwise, the complexity will prevent the venture from growing to any scale. The simplified model is a perfect way to disrupt clumsy, bloated incumbents who have grown up that way and pass on their inefficiencies to their customers.

TransferWise: Fintech Star Reimagining Money Transfers

We now are seeing the same Screwfix-like, low-end disruption take place in the finance industry. The perfect combination of a frustrated, unloved customer segment, lowering of regulatory barriers and ambitious entrepreneurs armed with technology and free-flowing capital has catapulted the financial technology (fintech) industry into the limelight. In areas such as money transfer, payments and property finance, digital disruptors have emerged and grown exponentially, taking profitable segments of customers away from banks.

The more we look at the successful fintech startups (if you can still call them that when some of them are valued at multiple billions of pounds) we see that their business model, entry, and growth strategies, fit well within the frameworks explained in this book.

TransferWise Disrupts the High-Barrier Banking Industry

TransferWise is a brilliant example of a tech startup that has disrupted the high-barrier banking industry. Founded in London in 2011, TransferWise set out to minimize bank fees on global money transfers. This was a time when banks blatantly charged their smaller customers 15% or more in fees, hidden charges, and exchange rates vastly different to the market rates. Hence, someone transferring just £500 could lose more than £75 in fees and other charges. Consumers were becoming aware of these fees as they could see the market exchange rates for the currencies they were transferring through Google and other foreign exchange quote sites.

Moreover, the banks made customers fill out long forms and visit their branches to do the transfer. Customers were frustrated and the banks didn't even realize this, as the person transferring £500 now and then is hardly a high-priority customer for the banks. This presented the perfect opportunity for a disruptor like TransferWise to serve this un-loved customer segment with a superior solution. TransferWise did just that by reducing transfer fees significantly and making the fees transparent.

Importantly, the whole money transfer process could be done easily and quickly online at its website or through its app, where customers were kept informed of the transfer status. When customers experienced money transfer through TransferWise, they became loyal and never went back to the 'old way' of doing money transfers.

As of quarter one, 2018, after only seven years in business, TransferWise has three million customers, transfers £2 billion every month to 69 countries in 47 currencies, and has grown to 1,000-plus employees in nine offices (Source: TransferWise UK, 2018).

TransferWise's approach of picking an existing but unloved segment of customers and delighting them with a superior solution works. Fortunately for aspiring entrepreneurs, the success process can be replicated for your own venture.

TransferWise's simplified model, which radically improves the customer journey and proposition, while keeping its operations simpler than the banks, has allowed it to significantly disrupt the retail foreign exchange market in several countries. Incumbents reliant on fat margins simply couldn't respond without destroying their businesses.

Like any orchestra that makes beautiful music, a tremendous amount of thought and work needs to go in before the music is heard and appreciated. The process becomes easier when the orchestra is resourced well with talented musicians and, importantly, plays together. We consider how to achieve this for any digital startup under 'What Resources Do You Need?' in the 'Execute' section of this book.

Resources

Customer Journey Mapping Tools

Customer journey mapping tools make it easier to produce and present your journey maps. They don't do the thinking or analysis for you but give you a canvas to work on. All the variants exist so that you can focus on the journey and are not worrying about drawing things out. Each one of the tools highlighted have particular strengths, and come in handy in different situations as explained below.

Smaply is a web-based customer journey mapping tool with a good visual interface. It is flexible enough for you create a journey bespoke to your industry and niche, and offers a free 14-day trial.

https://www.smaply.com/

Custellence is another web-based collaborative customer journey mapping tool. It is easy to use, and offers a free version with limited features.

https://custellence.com/

Lucidchart is a web-based general-purpose diagramming tool. It can be used to create customer journey maps; however, it isn't purpose built for journey maps.

https://www.lucidchart.com/blog/how-to-build-customer-journey-maps

Designing CX is a traditional paper-based innovation and journey mapping toolkit with many useful documents you can download. If you have a physical space where you can collaborate with your team to work through ideas and customer journeys over a period, the tools at Designing CX can be very valuable.

https://designingcx.com/

Software Product Design and Prototyping Tools and Services

InVision is a rapid design and prototyping tool that helps you create interactive mock-ups of your solution to get early feedback from potential users.

https://www.invisionapp.com/

Upwork is a marketplace to connect with freelance service providers. There are a vast number of design and product development experts from around the world. You can post your design or prototyping project on Upwork to find and select professionals who can build your initial designs or prototypes.

https://upwork.com

Useful Books

Oversubscribed is a relevant book by Daniel Priestley. Daniel states that the way to become oversubscribed is to be utterly remarkable in everything your business does. Designing your entire venture around the customer as we see in *Build the Right Thing* is a great start. *Oversubscribed* adds to this by helping you understand how customers behave. It explains how to leverage consumer behavior to become oversubscribed by having products or services that are worth talking about.

A satisfied customer is the best business strategy of all.

~ Michael LeBoeuf ~

EXECUTE

Chapter 3
What Resources Do You need?

It was a bleak, wintry day in central London, December 2016. Despite the miserable weather, 15 teams of entrepreneurs were in high spirits, gathered in a meeting room preparing to present to over 100 potential investors. Before the formal presentations began, there were networking opportunities for the entrepreneurs to pitch their ideas to potential investors. I was part of the Homegrown team. Though I'd been involved in startup fundraising meetings, as well as internal budget approvals, and had a track record of winning investments and internal funding, this set-up was a little unnerving. This was fundraising speed-dating style.

The venture capitalists in the room were mostly from well-known, reputable firms with recent track records of investing in technology startups. Beyond exchanging pleasantries and listening to our elevator pitch, the quality of their questions soon confirmed that this bunch were seasoned players in their game:

"If the CEO was hit by a bus tomorrow what would happen to your startup?"

"What is the one part of your system that competitors will take months to figure out and years to replicate?"

"Why are you doing this instead of sticking to a corporate job?"

After the formal presentation by each team, there were more similar questions from the audience. While processing the questions and answers, an insight surfaced, and the questions all made perfect sense.

During my MBA, one of my favorite topics was strategy. I was fortunate to have been able to interact with some of the brightest minds in the field, while at the Cranfield School of Management. A key part of the subject was practical exercises, which involved uncovering the real strategic assets within businesses: What are the factors that wins business? Is it its systems, processes, or its people and culture? I learnt and used tools that systematically dissect a business to arrive at the business's core strategic assets. A core strategic asset is one that wins business for that organization. Put another way, take the core strategic assets away from the business and soon it becomes unprofitable and dies.

Essentially, the theme of the questions being asked by the venture capitalists was trying to discover what the core strategic assets were in the startups they were considering funding.

This is fairly easy to comprehend if we look at McDonalds, which generates its massive revenues because it delivers consistent types of fast food through its standardized methods of procuring, storing, and cooking food. One of its core strategic assets is its processes. As a result of having these processes, it can replicate its product in any part of the world, hire almost anyone, and train them quickly to produce its food at its restaurants.

Whether you are a tech startup or a multibillion-dollar turnover corporation, there are always certain core strategic assets that help you win customers and sales. The money follows these assets and not the other way around.

If you are a digital startup, your core strategic assets will help you raise funding and attract the best talent to scale your business. It will then ensure a steady growth of customers and revenues so that you become a highly profitable business.

Larger organizations that are already profitable also depend on their core strategic assets to attract or retain customers and grow. A multimillion-pound construction materials business I worked with had some interesting core strategic assets. It surprised me that even with ageing IT systems, a mostly unskilled workforce, and a pretty average work culture, the business was able to attract multibillion pounds in annual sales and enjoy decent profitability.

To discover the core strategic assets, I asked myself: "What one or two things, if removed from this business, would cause it to grind to a halt?" The answer was easy to derive. The business had over 500 stores, which stocked cement, bricks, and other heavy building materials. These heavy materials were not profitable to deliver beyond a 30-mile radius and also required specialized lorries to load, transport, and unload the products. The business had built up its portfolio of stores over several decades. Access to markets through these properties was a key strategic asset. Secondly, it owned the specialized lorries required to transport these products to customers. Take those two things away and the business would grind to a halt quickly, quite literally.

All businesses need to have these core, strategic assets to exist. Your digital business needs them too. There are three types of core, strategic assets that you need to get right:
   a. Agile Mindset
   b. Agile Teams
   c. Agile Technology

When you execute your plan with these three strategic assets in place, your venture's chances of success increase dramatically. In the first two chapters we reached clarity on where and how to compete. That gives you direction; however, direction without energy doesn't get you to your destination. To get there you need energy, and the resources we cover in the next three chapters give you that energy.

"The money follows assets and not the other way around ."

~ Daniel Priestley ~

Chapter 4
Agile Mindset

What is the number-one resource required to launch and grow a successful startup? Many think it is access to capital and talent. Yet we now live in a world where knowledge, talent, and capital are easier to access than ever before. Yet many startups still fail. Why?

In my view, having worked with startups as well as large businesses, there is a common predictor of success. It is mindset; more specifically, the mindset of the founder and their team. Mindset isn't a tangible resource like capital or talent, yet it drives every decision, action, and outcome. Therefore, I've prioritized mindset as the most important of the resources needed in the execution phase.

In this chapter we will dive into the agile mindset required for your venture to thrive. By helping you understand why you are doing what you are doing, we will create energizing clarity and behaviors in you and your team, so you can head in the right direction and get to your destination.

The vast number of startups and digital transformation initiatives within large organizations don't meet their intended objectives, or they simply fail. While on the surface there could be reasons, such as market conditions, inadequate funding, or lack of skill sets, the real deeper reasons often lie in the teams not having had the right qualities and the associated behaviors. While we can go into a long list of human qualities that enable success, if we look at qualities and behaviors valuable to new initiatives, there are three qualities and four behaviors that stand out.

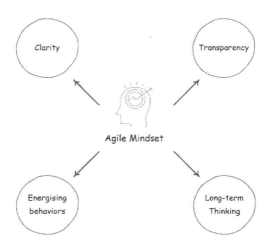

Clarity

Why Are You Doing This?

My Japanese colleagues were fond of visiting a place on the southern tip of Japan, Okinawa. The more I came to know of the place, the more it intrigued me, because Okinawa has the largest number of centenarians. In fact, living for over 100 years is quite common in Okinawa. There have been many studies trying to unravel the secrets of the longevity and good health of the people who live there, but few prove anything conclusive. However, there is one observation that stands out and contains valuable lessons for us as individuals in both our personal and professional lives. It has nothing to do with the food the people eat, the water, or anything physical. Rather, it has to do with something more intangible—mindset.

Okinawans refer to it as *ikigai*, which loosely translates into 'reason for being'.

It is easiest to think about *ikigai* as an intersection, the common ground between:

- What you are passionate about
- What you really care about
- What the world needs
- What you can get paid for

The concept of *ikigai* is summarized in the diagram below:

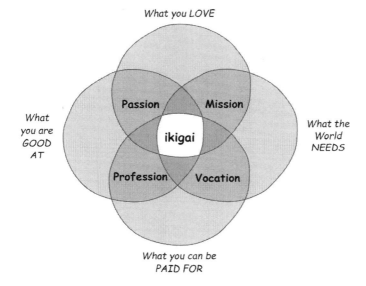

When you have tried to answer the above four questions, you will find that most of us are at the intersection of either two of the circles or, if we are lucky, at the intersection of three. Societal focus on material success means we have probably selected or fallen upon a career path that pays us the most and not necessarily makes us fulfilled or serves humanity. Moreover, few educational systems force us to think through the above questions and reach clarity before we embark on our careers. It seems different in Okinawa. Its residents are well versed in the concept of *ikigai*, either through formal education or through informal knowledge sharing. People take their time to discover the answers to the four questions. In fact, the process isn't rushed. The wise ones in Okinawa tell us that by not rushing the process, true answers reveal themselves in stages.

Ikigai helps you understand why you are doing what you are doing in the first place. It allows you to be clear about your own personal purpose. If you quickly find you don't love what you are trying to produce or are not particularly good at it, these are signs that your personal purpose may not align well with your venture's purpose. If, on the other hand, your personal purpose fits well with your own venture, you will sense this quite clearly too.

Why Is This Important?

Have you ever interacted with a business where you immediately sensed that those involved were not trying very hard to make you as the customer happy? I certainly have. If the team that drives a business isn't engaged, customers sense that mediocre experience immediately, and the team derives its behaviors from its leader.

If you are the leader of your new venture, or a key player in it, unless you passionately love what you do you run out of steam quickly. On the contrary, loving what you do creates more energy for you and keeps you energized over time. Importantly, the increase in your energy and happiness does something else fundamentally important to succeed in your mission. It is contagious. It energizes not just you but the team you will need to attract and retain in order to complete your mission.

So, take your time to figure out your *ikigai*. It is time well invested. You may not have all the answers to start with. That is fine too. Plant the questions in your mind. Answers will start to emerge over time and your personal why will become clear.

Some of us who are new to the concept of *ikigai* may struggle with the idea of aspiring for clarity yet tolerating ambiguity. Therein lies the duality of life—just as light follows darkness, peaks follow valleys, and sound follows silence—answers follow questions.

A truly agile mindset is purpose-driven yet, at the same time, it isn't rushing to achieve anything. *Ikigai* allows you to discover your purpose and sows the seeds of an agile mindset. You will naturally feel receptive and open to receive these answers as they arise and start putting the puzzle together, revealing the grand picture.

So, what's the link between *ikigai* and longevity? Simple. Understanding your internal purpose creates all the energy one needs to sustain life. The Indian yogic philosophy aligns with this thinking as well. One who discovers a higher purpose and is driven to make a positive impact in society gets all the energy they require to make that happen, and to not just survive but thrive. This happens naturally. People race the sun to start the day when they have a mission. We have all experienced it.

The work we have done in the earlier chapters allows us to answer the questions such as where we are competing as a business and how we are going to do that. *Ikigai* is a personal version of that same process. Your personal why. In my own experience, having observed both startups and projects within large organizations, the number-one resource to get things done is mindset, specifically an agile mindset. It is the fuel that provides the energy to navigate the bumps, humps, and hurdles to reach your destination.

Sadly, what we often see is the opposite. Entrepreneurs start on a venture because it is the coolest thing to do at that moment, or venture capitalists are throwing millions at a particular emerging sector and the entrepreneur wants a part of the action. You hear this often in startup pitches for funding. These pitches talk about a cool technology solution for large markets run by a fantastic team of Harvard graduates with blue chip work experience.

So, if all magical ingredients are there, why aren't many of these startups becoming runaway successes making a meaningful impact on humanity? It is the missing part that always intrigues me—the lack of purpose. The lack of purpose that is driving the venture is conspicuously absent. This often starts with the founder. Ray Dalio is an American billionaire hedge fund manager who founded Bridgewater Associates, which managed over US$125 billion in 2018. His book, *Principles: Life and Work*, is a window into how a purpose and principle-driven life leads to extraordinary results.

Are You at One with Your Environment?

When your personal why starts to get clearer and aligns with your venture's purpose, you and your team have a destination. People who find themselves in such a situation then intuitively go on to create a plan to get to their destination. This may involve building a detailed business plan, which has perfect answers to everything that will happen in terms of growth until the business reaches an exit. If it is a project within a large corporation then managers set about creating a detailed project plan with beautiful Gantt charts, outlining each task and the completion date. They commit to a completion date within a specified budget as well. This makes everyone feel good because they can report a clear plan to upper management.

In reality though, both the startup plan and the corporate project plan are doomed to fail from the outset. The reasons are not difficult to understand. Both exercises are at best a speculation of what may happen assuming that the organizer of the initiative has control over many external events. At worst, these are outright lies to make the organizers look good or retain their job, at least in the short term.

Believing one of these plans is the same as believing a pilot who claims to know exactly how the wind will blow from minute to minute throughout the flight. Really, nobody knows. However, the pilot doesn't doubt that they will reach the destination because they know that they have to make thousands of corrections during the flight to keep the plane on course. After the pilot has reached a safe altitude, they set the plane on autopilot and the plane makes the necessary corrections to keep itself stable and on course towards its waypoints and destination. This is how successful businesses are built and projects delivered: the mindset involved welcomes changes as part of completing the journey.

The autopilot analogy also provides an insight into another key aspect of the agile mindset. To keep the plane flying stably and on course, the autopilot system relies on real-time input. Sensors around the plane tell it how high and at what angle it is flying. The input then leads to corrective actions to change the heading or angle at which the plane is travelling. In essence, the plane is aware of its situational context and taking ongoing actions based on that information. This subtle process that happens constantly is taken for granted when you are a passenger. However, imagine if the autopilot system isn't getting the inputs to be aware of the plane's height, heading, or angle. Repeated small changes in heading can take the plane to Canada when it was meant to be heading for New York, or worse, it could crash.

An agile mindset constantly scans the external environment to understand the current context; not the one that has passed or the one that is coming, but this one, the current one. The second part of the mindset is to accept that reaction to the context is necessary. Not by reflex but by deliberate processing of the input.

This clarity of internal purpose, ongoing understanding of context, and deliberate reaction to that information are traits of winning individuals and teams. The struggle that many go through in trying to reach their desires can be avoided with these mindsets. As with most things in life, the things that work are simple but not necessarily perceived as easy. They become immensely easier once we make a start, just like the pilot who gets their plane to take off and gets it into autopilot mode.

Transparency

All Hearing, All Seeing Teams

The purpose of this book is to help entrepreneurs and managers think through and create winning digital strategies and to 'build the right thing'. However, only when a team is involved can anything meaningful or large-scale be achieved. The challenge in having a group of people is that we are now dealing with people who all want to do their own things. This is where the team members need to be transparent with each other. Internal transparency arises from understanding the benefit of sharing information. Lack of internal transparency, on the other hand, causes confusion, fear, misgivings, and low energy within the team. In the teams I build I ensure that every team member can articulate the business strategy, how the business helps our target customers, and how we go about doing things. When leaders achieve unified responses, they can be sure that their teams are now aligned in purpose and execution. Complete internal transparency is no longer a nice to have, but a hygiene factor to succeed.

Achieving this transparency, especially in a corporate environment, is more challenging than in a startup. The startup is more likely to be forming its new team with a clear objective from the outset, all being driven by the leader. If the leader is insecure, opaque, and reserved, then they are unlikely to go far in attracting a team to start with. Generally, in a startup, there tends to be less politics and siloed working because the few people involved have organized themselves into a cross-functional product team focused on customers.

Larger corporate organizations that are facing digital transformation have more challenges on the team front because of traditional siloed structures. Much of how we organize businesses today is a remnant from an industrial age where people were assigned to specialized functions to divide and complete the task. The siloed structures of operations, finance, IT, and human resources worked in a non-digital era where the pace of change was manageable and predictable. However, digitization has rendered those models increasingly obsolete. Today's leading businesses have technology at their core. Amazon thinks of itself as a technology company that happens to be selling things. Google is a technology company that has redefined the entire media landscape. Recent successes, such as Spotify, TransferWise, and Alibaba are all, at their heart, tech companies involved in different industries, such as media, retail, and commerce.

These modern companies get their most ambitious initiatives done, launched, and developed through mission-driven product teams that contain people from various disciplines, such as technology, design, product management, operations, and finance. One reason for doing this is to break silos, but also, more importantly, to create internal transparency; not just PowerPoint-based token transparency done at information sharing sessions, but instant and total transparency that forces everyone in the team to share what they know in order to achieve what needs to be done—in short, productive transparency. This combination of a well-defined mission, some healthy time pressure, and a cross-functional team with differing but complementary skill sets, almost naturally induces behaviors that encourage internal transparency.

So, why am I not throwing in another management buzzword such as cooperation, team players, or engagement here? Aren't successful outcomes attained when people within a team cooperate? Decades of management thinking, time, and money has been wasted in getting people to cooperate. Running offsite team-building sessions to get people to interact in informal settings did little for productivity other than people now being more relaxed about doing things than they were before.

Things started to change when management thinkers understood that transparent teams cooperated naturally. Transparency in teams and organizations encourages cooperation naturally. I understood this when I worked in Tokyo. Those of us who have interacted with Japanese people would understand that Japan is a high-trust society, both in personal and professional interactions. This means most communications within teams can be taken at face value.

As part of my work in Japan, I was involved in various software development teams, which were spun up to deliver client projects. It always fascinated me how quickly the teams became productive and started delivering working software. Usually, a team would be formed, and a stand-up meeting held to introduce the team members in the morning. The meeting rarely lasted more than an hour. On the same day, you would see the team engaged in productive one-to-one discussion to understand, clarify, and find various solutions. Within days, you could see the team coming together energetically to solve complex problems, and someone new walking into the room where the team was working would have thought that this team had been on the job for months based on their cooperative behaviors.

In my work across the globe, I also encountered various other software development teams. Invariably, they often took significantly longer to become productive than the Japanese teams I'd worked with. They often went through the forming, storming, norming, performing phases taught in project management courses.

It took me a while to understand why:

Trust leads to Transparency, which leads to Cooperation

Transparency is a behavior that sits between the quality of trust and the action of cooperation. Trust leads to transparency, which brings about cooperation.

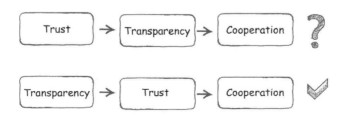

Management thinking has, after much expense and time, learnt that you can neither induce trust nor cooperation. After all, how many times have you trusted something based on someone telling you to trust that thing? However, we have learnt that by affecting the behavior of transparency, we can grow trust and induce cooperation. Businesses have often tried to affect employee behaviors by having the right leader. Where there is a strong, dynamic leader, the team mimics their behaviors and hence achieves success. The challenge with strong dynamic leaders is that they are rare and difficult to find. If you are lucky enough to find them, how do you have them available in sufficient numbers required? Internal transparency is a lot easier to achieve within teams and more reliable as a predictor of cooperation and success. Hence, the modern focus on transparent teams, and we consider how to quickly create transparent teams in a subsequent chapter.

The fact that teams that cooperate are significantly more successful than those that don't isn't a cliché. There is sound economic rationale for this. It is predicated on the economic theory of comparative advantage. This theory proved mathematically that two parties in a trade are better off when they specialize in a specific area and trade that specialty. Think Germany and car production, India and software outsourcing, or China and manufacturing. Here each of these countries are specializing in a sector and trading that expertise with the rest of the world. It has been proven that specializing and trading leads to prosperity for the nations involved.

For success and prosperity, both need to be true; that is, each country needs to specialize and also trade. Just specializing and not trading, or trading without specializing doesn't cut it.

The same logic applies to individuals. In a team that comprises skilled specialists (such as software engineers, designers, finance professionals, and product managers), and where there is transparent cooperation between these skilled professionals, the odds of success are tilted significantly in the team's favor.

Do You Know How the World Sees You?

High-performing, successful ventures are not just internally transparent, they are transparent with their external environment. After all, the customer is increasingly an extension of the team and the most important source of feedback. The customer votes with their wallet, and the business is made or broken based on their reactions.

Successful ventures put the customer at the heart of their business. From strategy, to team structures, operations, and support services, all decision-making is organized around the customer's mission and journey. There is frequent engagement at various levels of the organization with real customers, not focus groups or paid surveys, but real customers. This is an extension of the internal transparency to the external. In fact, over time, the boundaries between internal and external stakeholders become blurred.

I recently collaborated on a project with commercetools, a tech company that makes modern e-commerce software. The company invites its customers for a product planning meeting every quarter. During the two days in which this happens, members of the product development team (comprising its technical leads and product owners) actively develop the product roadmap based on the customer input. After the session, the company releases new features developed during the roadmap session. The frequent release of new features increases customer loyalty, as the software becomes more valuable and encourages more feedback, reinforcing the positive loop. What is interesting in the roadmapping session is that there is a high level of external transparency and openness. The customer provides real feedback on what they have discovered while using the software. The company then ideates solutions and discusses with the customer before converging on a feature to be developed. Where there is no strategic fit for the company to develop a particular feature, there is a frank conversation as to why it isn't the right thing for the company to do.

This company has been growing exponentially during the past year and taking significant market share in the crowded e-commerce software space, often winning business away from opaque, slow to react tech giants. In the current digital age, we are faced with unprecedented access to information. Businesses can no longer operate opaque models that keep customers in the dark. Successful, modern businesses are co-creating their solutions, commercial offer, and product development with their customers. All it takes is a clear, open mindset to capitalize on the vast opportunities, both internal and external, that transparency can bring.

Long-Term Thinking

Successful startups understand that they own the overall experience for all their customers, employees, financiers, and partners. Decisions are driven by the customers' and other stakeholders' experiences more than other considerations such as cost or time. It is about getting things right in both the short and long term, i.e. building the right thing, and not about egotistical races to superficially complete 'projects' within impossible timescales.

Successful teams approach delivery of software products as an ongoing, never-ending process. The work may be more intense at the onset and ad hoc when the product is in use and scales up. However, it is not a project that finishes. There is long-term thinking about both the customers' and the team's experience. Many entrepreneurs make the mistake of trying to deliver perfection for the customer but ruthlessly wearing down their own team with impossible demands and timescales. This doesn't work. Successful leaders recognize that joyful teams deliver far better customer experiences than any world-class but miserable teams. The beginning and end here are inclusive of everyone who contributes, not just the ones wielding power through title or money.

Jeff Bezos, who founded Amazon, understood this, and organized his business accordingly, around long-term teams that continuously work on customer-centric products. He then supported the teams by removing the pressures that come with trying to pay shareholder dividends. Instead, he invested back into his products and teams. Ultimately, shareholders who forewent small dividends have now reaped enormous returns in Amazon's exponential stock price growth.

Anything yields to the individual whose mind focuses on it. It may not happen immediately, but it inevitably does over time. Hence, everyone is better off when we gaze into the long term and align our product and venture accordingly.

Energizing Behaviors

The output of a productive agile mindset can be observed in the productive behaviors of the individual. While there are a range of behaviors, in my observation, only four are most relevant. Successful entrepreneurs and teams exhibit these four behaviors:

1. Fearless and Fast
2. Entrepreneurially Driven / Creativity
3. Data Driven (Right data to right decisions) / Humility
4. Frugal

Fearless and Fast

If you have decided to climb Mount Everest and are sitting at the foot of the mountain looking at its sheer height and steepness, listening to tales of the hundreds of climbers who have died in their attempts to climb it, whose bodies you will probably see on the way up, the chances are you are not going to get far on your ascent. You could sit at the base of the mountain and worry your entire life away, listening to that little voice in your head come up with arguments as to the perils of climbing the mountain. Sadly, that same little voice will also come up with counter arguments as to why you should attempt the climb and about the glory that will be yours. The only thing that happens as you sit there, listening to this little voice of arguments and counter arguments, is fear takes over. Fear may completely paralyze you, so you drop the idea altogether. The reality is that the idea doesn't drop you. It will haunt you for the rest of your life that you didn't go forward with your dream.

Almost without fail, all the successful entrepreneurs I've met, or the managers who made a difference in large corporations, tend to be fearless, at least when it comes to executing new initiatives. They don't worry too much about all that can go wrong with the initiative. Rather, they evaluate their strategies, make an informed decision as to the odds of their success, and get started. They recognize that fear is an illusion that stops action. Consider all the many things you have feared in life that never came to pass.

I was once asked to be part of a team that undertook due diligence on a possible acquisition target. The acquiring company was a large telecommunication multinational that I was working with. The target company was an Indian IT service provider with mostly telecom operators as its customers. This business had grown to employ around 2,000 people globally in under seven years, and had built an enviable client list, and there were good synergies for my company to acquire this fast-growing business. Through the due diligence process, my admiration for this business grew, as evidence unfolded of their bold expansion, while providing a valued service for their customers.

In due course, the business was indeed acquired and, in the process of integrating the acquired business into our own, I got to know the management team. During our first meeting, the key managers within the acquired business were invited to our offices in Singapore to explore how to integrate and support each other's businesses to grow further. The managers explained their business in detail and shared plans for future growth. We exchanged many ideas and agreed on some next steps.

Throughout the due diligence process, I'd had a burning question that I still longed to know the answer to during this initial meeting. Due to Asian business meeting protocols, I dare not ask the question because I was junior to most of the managers present. The question, though, was simple: why had this particular company succeeded in attracting the attention of a global telecom giant, who then went on to acquire them at a premium? There were many similar businesses being run out of India, with similar models and similar management teams. I convinced myself that this company had simply been lucky.

At the end of the meeting I saw the visiting team to the lift as is customary in Japanese business etiquette, where one should wait until the guests' lift has arrived and the doors have closed. The deputy CEO, who had been in the meeting with us, got into the lift and faced me. He held the lift door briefly to prevent it from closing and looked me in the eye. Then he calmly uttered a sentence that has stayed with me since then and affected many of my decisions.

"Haja, we were fearless." The lift door closed, and I've never seen him since.

With those four words he answered that burning question I'd had all along. To this day I've never known how he knew my question.

Deep inside I know that was the genuine reason why this company had attracted the attention of the telecom giant, over all other similar businesses.

It is fearlessness that makes ordinary teams pull away from the pack and become unstoppable, winning teams. Fearless honesty with customers and colleagues, fearlessness in any situation, fearlessness of the consequences of trying, fearlessness of what the world may think, reward you with, or punish you for. Fear is draining, but action cures fear.

In our modern world, the economics of society means that there is often a heavy penalty for failure. Entrepreneurs can lose everything and be ruined financially, managers can wreck careers that have been built over decades, and both will have to face a society that values winning. In this context fear can be real. However, greatness often lies beyond, when you are willing to look past fear.

Fearlessness makes you attractive in an energizing way. Teams and money almost seem to find you and want to support you to achieve your goals.

Once you have tasted fearlessness, it is unlikely you will cower back into your previous place of comfort. When you become fearless in your actions, you naturally speed up. Quite simply, you are not wasting time worrying about the consequences but are taking action and more action. This leads to results and encourages you to repeat the process, even more fearlessly. The wasted time spent in fear can now be spent on creativity, which you will agree can never be a waste.

Entrepreneurial Drive and Creativity

You are more than likely reading this book because you want to improve something. The chapters on where and how you compete are an exercise in how you can create value for your target customers. If you are trying to do that you would fit well within the economist Joseph Schumpeter's definition that "an entrepreneur is a force of industrial mutation that incessantly revolutionizes the economic structure from within, incessantly destroying the old one, incessantly creating a new one."

The entrepreneur's drive comes from their dissatisfaction with the status quo and the deeply held belief that things can be different and better. Successful entrepreneurs constantly and pervasively create. They don't stop at just creating the core product, but are creative with every aspect of the business. They reimagine how they recruit, motivate talent and partners, innovate how they raise finance, and the list goes on.

They are curious about and question every aspect of their environment. Where there is sufficient evidence that a new approach is required, they don't think twice about creating one. However, we should not mistake the rebels of the business world, armed with books, blog articles, and a bad attitude, with genuine change makers. If you are a rebel who has something negative to say about everything and cannot conceive something better, you wouldn't quite fit the bill of an entrepreneur, never mind a successful one.

Whatever idea for a venture you have is likely to be a change, and change is *only* accepted if you can influence people to accept it. To do that you must exhibit grace in your discontentment.

When Mr. Lee Hsien Long, the Prime Minister of Singapore, ended one of his national day addresses by wishing for every Singaporean to be 'gracefully discontented', he summed up beautifully Singapore's success. Respectfully challenging the status quo with the right research, data, and a positive vision is how Singapore is led. The long-term success of many of Singapore's businesses is testament to the success of graceful discontentment.

Humility—Let the Data Speak

This brings us to the third productive behavior. A data-driven approach.

As a venture takes shape and gathers momentum, the leader and their team need to make many small but correct decisions, just like the plane on autopilot, to keep flying. The pace of competition and complex environments mean the leader should constantly make decisions based on data, and continuously challenge the data. Using purely instinct-based decision-making will lead to relying on chance. On the other hand, purely relying on data would lead to 'analysis paralysis', where one can dive deeper and deeper and end up with nothing at the end, having wasted lots of time.

The trick is to use data sufficiently to avoid bad decisions. Data is vague in identifying what you need to do but very good at telling you what you should *not* be doing. I often joke with my teams that data analysis tells you very well who you should not marry but doesn't really tell you who you can have a happy marriage with.

If you can avoid bad decisions, that is more than half the battle won. Preventing the negative, draining experience that results from bad decisions frees us up to make the good ones.

Humility plays a strong role in getting value out of data. We tend to see the world through our own lens. No two people interpret the same data in the same way, purely because they are filtering the data through their own perceptions and life experiences. This makes for strange situations when two people look at the same data and have quite differing interpretations. Both would argue their viewpoint, and one of two things may happen. If they value the outcome over the relationship with the other person, they will stick to their own interpretation. If they value the relationship over the outcome, both will agree a muddled compromise on the interpretation. Neither approach is the best outcome.

Looking at the data with humility and trying to understand what is actually there and what we think should be there takes some mindfulness and practice. People I've worked with who successfully adopt a data-driven approach, accept the data for what it is truly showing, not what they wish it showed. Too often we are embedded in a mindset where data is a supporting tool for our ambitions, where we use the facts that support our case, and conveniently leave out the ones that don't. Observe the data with humility and curiosity and it will be far more valuable in helping form reliably good decisions. When you are running a new venture, there are very few times you can afford to make bad decisions.

Frugal

Successful initiatives often mask an overlooked element—being frugal. This element isn't easily observed from the outside because it involves not doing certain things. It is about being frugal and resourceful rather than being conspicuously wasteful. It is also rooted in the earlier part of the strategy process, that is, if your venture is creating value for your target customers, then those potential customers recognize this and are drawn to use your product and also talk about it and spread the word. There is no need for overpriced, self-promoting publicity to drive growth. Rather, operate frugally and strive for natural organic growth, which creates sufficient cash flow and profits to fund the business.

This frugality and resourcefulness isn't limited to just attracting customers but to all aspects of the business, from procurement to managing overheads. In a world where it seems venture capital is abundantly available, this idea may seem old-fashioned. Why be frugal when everyone else is splurging and there is plenty of venture capital cash to be spent? The answer lies in the fact that digital has changed the basic economics of industries forever and when we understand how, we will appreciate that frugality is a necessity to win in this new world.

There are two major economic forces that digital has unleashed. Firstly, the digital transformation of an industry often benefits the consumers and not the businesses involved in that industry. This means the consumer often gets a lower price for the same service or product and is better off, while the business and the overall industry makes a lower total profit. This happens because digital strips out non-value-adding parts of an industry. As a result of consumers being able to book directly with airlines, middlemen such as travel agents with physical presence have been taken out of the value chain and have all but disappeared. With low-cost airlines even avoiding online travel sites, they pass the savings to the passengers and compete more aggressively with national airlines, wiping many of them out. Similarly, a taxi ride costs less with Uber than with a radio taxi in most cities. Passengers once again benefit from the savings, while many taxi companies are being forced out of business. In the hotel sector, Airbnb now offers alternative accommodation to traditional hotel chains, often at much more competitive prices. While guests pay less, traditional hotel chains' profits have dropped.

Despite digital transformations shifting value to consumers, incumbents who undertake successful digital transformations can wipe out slow-to-change businesses within their industry. Walmart is a great example of an incumbent threatened by digital players, such as Amazon, which has radically transformed itself digitally to achieve relevance and sustained growth.

The second economic impact of digital is that winners in an industry take all, leaving very little for competitors. Prior to digitization, it was common to see several large players within an industry. However, the low cost of moving to a digital supplier meant consumers could easily drop old buying habits and move to a new digital player. Amazon, Uber, and Airbnb all benefited from this low switching cost. The net result is that digital disruptors can scale their customer base beyond traditional boundaries, such as geographies, and corner entire industries. Customers flock to the business that provides the greatest value. While the cheapest price doesn't represent the greatest value, a competitive price is a requirement before other factors such as convenience can be overlaid.

To provide competitive value, the venture must be lean in all its cost centers to make a profit and grow organically. The other option is to forsake profitability and fuel growth through venture funding, hoping to corner the market. Amazon seems to have done this by not bothering about profits and focusing on growth at all costs. However, if you are starting a new digital venture, you are unlikely to be in Amazon's shoes, so there is real benefit to focusing on the bottom line for a simple reason. If you are profitable you can wait out growth, and the ride is far more enjoyable for you and your team. On the other hand, if you are bleeding money, you are on borrowed time, the pressure is enormous, and it often leads to bad decisions. If you are backed by external funding and bleeding money, it isn't a great place to be in mentally and emotionally. It is better to fuel a profitable venture through external funding than to try to make one profitable.

There is also an unexpected benefit to frugality—it gives you satisfaction. While the strategies to differentiate and attract new customers ups your chances of success, there are no guarantees. There are many variables, such as external market forces and consumer behavior, on which you have little or no control. However, you often have control over the cost structure of your enterprise.

If you are a manager in a corporation launching a new venture, you will often be given a budget and it is in your interest to manage that wisely and increase the time you have to get your initiative to profit. Too often, new initiatives within corporations are stopped not because they are failing, but because they have run out of budget.

Frugality allows you to reach break-even and profitability faster. If you are profitable you can wait out growth. Time works in your favor. If you are making losses, time works against you. Frugality buys you time.

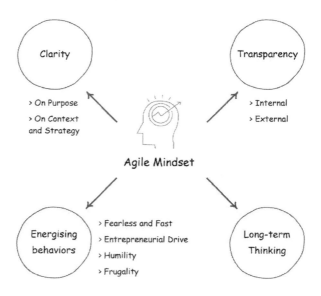

We have seen that the agile mindset begins with understanding why you are doing what you are doing. When you are doing what you love and can align that with your venture, you are energized. This in turn attracts the right team to execute your vision. Once you are on your way, remaining tuned into the external environment, learning, and adapting using data as feedback is vital to growth. This clarity gives you and your team direction and keeps you on course, but to function as a highly effective team you need to be brutally transparent, both within the team and to the external world. This encourages trust and cooperative behaviors, which are both vital for you to keep growing.

Now you not only *have* direction but have started *moving* in the right direction. To reach your destination, and to surmount the many obstacles that may come your way, you need energy. The right behaviors produce this energy. Being fearless and fast, entrepreneurially driven, and creative, being humble enough to make data-driven decisions, and exercising frugality are energizing behaviors, which increase the chances of you getting to your destination.

In today's world, knowledge is more abundant and accessible than ever before. It is no longer for the privileged few. Anyone who wants to start out and make a new venture succeed has access to the knowledge they need. However, not everyone will hit their targets. Those with the right agile mindset will significantly increase their odds of success. They will also impart this mindset to their teams. We explore how in the next section.

Resources

Principles by Ray Dalio is a good read to develop a clear success-oriented mindset rather than bowing to conventional wisdom. Ray Dalio is one of the world's most successful investors and entrepreneurs. In his book, he shares the unconventional principles that helped him create unique results in life and business. The book and other related content are available for free through his website. https://www.principles.com/

Trillion Dollar Coach is a management lessons playbook from legendary coach and business executive Bill Campbell, whose mentoring of some of the most successful modern entrepreneurs from Google and Apple has helped create well over a trillion dollars in market value. It contains useful examples of scenarios that most startups will face when scaling the business, hiring, and managing talent.

The Art of Thinking Clearly by Rolf Dobelli is an eye-opening look at human psychology and reasoning. Before you develop an agile mindset in yourself and your teams, this book can help clear the existing clutter, help avoid 'cognitive errors', and help you to make better choices in all aspects of life.

Intelligence is the ability to adapt to change.

~ Stephen Hawking ~

Chapter 5
Agile Team

Every successful entrepreneur points to their great team as a key reason for their success. There is a saying that if you want to go fast you go it alone, but if you want to go far you go as a group. In most circumstances, a business that succeeds in a competitive marketplace is simply a better-performing team than the other teams that play in that same space. The vision and drive may come from the leader, but it takes a great team to make that vision become reality. If you are striving to achieve success in a new initiative, be it in an entrepreneurial startup or a venture within a large corporation, it is likely that you have already understood that it is great teams that help you reach your end vision.

Yet I've seen first-hand so many startups and initiatives fail spectacularly because they cannot get their teams right. In fact, not forming the right team to execute the mission is probably the number one reason why entrepreneurs and managers fail to deliver on their vision. Repeatedly I hear from them that they struggled to attract, retain, and motivate the right talent to get the job done.

On the other hand, those who go on to achieve great success have mastered the art of attracting the right talent, keeping them productive over a long period, and motivating them effectively. Yet is this really an art? Having worked with these successful entrepreneurs and managers, the formula for forming great teams is relatively straightforward, but of course, as with all simple things, execution isn't easy.

In this chapter I summarize the insights of several successful entrepreneurs and managers on forming great agile teams, having spent time with them (as well as some who have not quite hit their intended mark). I've also taken into consideration my own experience in both startups and large corporations around the world, as well as the latest research on organizational behavior from thought leaders such as McKinsey.

Forming and growing teams in a startup is rather different to doing the same in a large corporation. Nevertheless, there are valuable lessons for each other, and I share these here in this chapter. Then, when both teams have got customer traction and are trying to scale up their venture, the team dynamics are similar. In this chapter we will look into:

- Team foundations – success qualities required for any team
- The basics of an agile team
- Startup teams – how to form them, get them aligned on your blueprint, and execute
- Corporate digital transformation and new venture teams – how these teams differ to startups
- Teams for scale-ups – how to form growth-oriented teams

How many times have you heard a startup entrepreneur enthuse about the great teams they are going to form, and their agile and joyful ways of working? I've never heard this. However, every entrepreneur I've met tried to convince me how great their idea was and how it would change the world. Ideas do not change the world—people do. More specifically, great teams who execute great ideas do. Yet finding these great people, getting them excited about your great idea, and getting them to execute is such a challenge. Not thinking about forming and motivating teams is a real blind spot in every new venture. Let's see through real-world examples how this blind spot plays out and how we fix it before you even hire your first team member.

The People Blind Spot

I first met Andy at a startup pitching event where entrepreneurs pitch their business to potential investors with the aim of raising capital. His idea was simple: Andy had developed a hardware and software solution to solve the key handover process in Airbnb rentals. His app and lock allowed guests to check themselves into their rental by controlling the door remotely through a smart lock and app. Andy pitched the idea and opportunity very effectively, and at the end of the presentations there was a long queue of potential investors and partners wanting to talk to him.

I watched his progress from the sidelines and met up with him about two years after the startup event. He told me how his venture took off spectacularly because he attracted all the money he needed to launch his startup, and then how it all quickly fell apart. Andy struggled to deliver the product and make it a commercial success, even though there was a strong demand. Unfortunately, competitors who started much later, with significantly less funding and an inferior product, went on to overtake him and capture the market space.

I asked Andy what he thought was the main reason for the lack of growth when he had the right product and the right funding. After what seemed like a long pause, he admitted that his number one reason for not getting to the growth stage, and then having to wind up his startup, was the fact that he couldn't attract the right talent. If he did manage to attract the right talent, he couldn't keep them motivated to adapt to the rapidly changing market to meet his customers' needs. I probed further and asked him why that had happened. His response, like many other entrepreneurs who have had a similar experience, was quite expected.

Andy had focused on hiring bright talent for his startup. This often means trying to hire bright software engineers, at high salaries, who have delivered challenging solutions in previous roles. In addition, he needed to attract the right marketing people to sell the product in a cost-effective manner. Andy found himself competing with equally well-funded startups and tech giants for the same talent, and soon realized it was a seller's market. Every capable engineer he interviewed had at least two or three job offers by the end of the recruitment process and he often had to settle for hiring the second or third best.

While he thought he had better luck with the marketing team, he faced a different kind of a challenge. More people applied for the marketing roles. However, the kind of people who showed up in response to his advertisements hardly had the relevant experience or the pedigree to give him confidence that they would succeed in a team game. Hence, Andy ended up hiring his second or third choice employees on both the tech and marketing fronts. He thought he could make do with them, convinced that his exciting startup mission would bring out the best in his new team. However, competing egos, basic lack of a team culture, and not understanding the real purpose of the business meant the team was performing well below its potential. The sum was significantly less than its parts.

To his credit, Andy has had enough time to reflect on his own contribution to this outcome. Prior to the startup, he was a successful rising star within a well-known technology company. However, he was a bit of a rebel, with his own strong views on how things should be done. He had long dreamt of starting his own venture, so that he didn't need to convince the people around him to buy in to his idea and support him. Strangely, he found this very rebellious streak within the kind of people he hired in his startup. Lack of leadership experience and not understanding the tools to persuade each team member to pull in the same direction, contributed to him being dragged into weak micro-management rather than coaching and motivating.

Andy's story is so frighteningly common in the startup world, where the talent challenge is very real. If the startup has a clear vision and some funding driven by a capable founder, it can attract some talent. However, the challenge arises when forming a high-performing team that sustains its direction and drive to finish the mission. The uncertainties of a startup mean enormous pressures on individuals when things don't quite work. The ever-looming threat of running out of funding, new product releases not gaining customer traction, and long hours to make all of these things right does take a severe toll on most team members.

My own experience in the corporate world taught me lessons that can be useful to startups. In the corporate world, the business is already well past the startup stage and has a strong employer brand, and in theory it is easier to attract talent. However, the dilemma in the corporate world is that often there isn't an exciting challenge to make the most out of the talent.

Recently, I led the digital transformation of a large corporation in the UK with over £2 billion in annual turnover. Working with the top team, I'd put together a digital transformation plan. We tested ideas from the plan in an agile way and the results were highly encouraging. The reason for this was that the business was in the building materials distribution industry, and digital innovation has been lacking throughout that industry for many years. As such, even small incremental innovations in digital tools were welcomed by its customer base, who were used to similar technological conveniences in other sectors, such as retail. One of the biggest challenges of this digital transformation was attracting the right talent. It was quite clear from the onset that the business had not historically attracted talent that would help deliver a major digital transformation. Secondly, the location of its headquarters, about 100 miles north of London, made it difficult to build large-scale digital teams, because much of the UK's technology talent is concentrated in London. Even with a global brand, exciting digital transformation plans, generous compensation, and full management support, we struggled for many months to build the right team required to deliver the full digital transformation.

Over time I discovered the reasons why this had happened. Firstly, the type of people who were attracted to a startup had different aspirations compared to those who would seek out a large stable business. Even when the large business had ambitious digital aspirations, the perception among the recruits was that corporations are not where digital innovations happen. Additionally, the ideal recruits in the digital space have several opportunities open to them. It is easier than ever to join a startup and get the same salary as in a large corporation, and equity options on top of that. If the startup succeeds there is usually a large financial pay-out and a feeling of pride. If it folds, there isn't much downside, and the resumé, ironically, may become more valuable due to that entrepreneurial experience. The ability to make a large difference in a small team within a startup, compared to making a small difference in a large team, draws many people towards the new ventures.

Nevertheless, both situations, whether you are building a startup team or a new venture within a large corporation, can offer exciting opportunities. If the business has the right product, financial backing, and a good founding team, it is possible to attract some amazing talent and motivate them to deliver game-changing business. Similarly, corporate managers, if bold, can tap into the enormous creativity and drive offered by those who have run startups to launch and deliver their own corporate ventures.

Regardless of the situation, the founder or manager is trying to build a high-performing team that is aligned to the vision and strategy, owns the customer experience, and continuously improves the product. We explore how to achieve a high-performing team in the following sections.

Due to the challenges of building a high-performing technology team, a common mistake that both entrepreneurs and managers make is to outsource the problem to either IT service providers, management consultants, or early-stage product development companies. While these agents are highly competent at selling their services into the businesses, repeatedly we have seen that they are unable to deliver the ongoing product development and customer traction required for the venture to succeed. It isn't difficult to see why this happens. From the onset there is a conflict of interest; the agent makes more revenues based on a long-term engagement with the client. There is no alignment of interests, and the teams that are recruited are not behind the founder's vision and strategy; they have very little to lose if they don't deliver. It is always better to have a smaller team whose interests are fully aligned with the venture, rather than a large team with impressive CVs and a conflict of interest.

There are three distinct teams:

- Those who are driving an independent startup
- Those who are driving a venture within a large corporation
- Those who have gone past startup stage and are scaling up the business, either in a startup or in a large corporation

Each of these three distinct teams have different needs and characteristics. Before I share with you the approach that works to form, engage, and motivate these teams to align with the strategy you have created, there are some irrefutable laws for teams. These are the basic foundational qualities for any team to operate. Let's dive into these first.

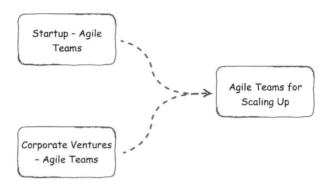

Team Foundations

Regardless of the stage your team is at, be it startup or scale-up, or the context under which it is operating, be it a funded startup or corporate venture, there are four foundations you need to get right:

1. Interest alignment
2. Customer centricity
3. Living agile
4. Playing a team game

Interest Alignment

If you don't get anything else right with the team you are forming, ensure there is interest alignment. I cannot stress this strongly enough. The interest of the individual and the objectives of the venture need to be aligned. What that interest is depends on the specific situation. Ways the individual members of the team and the person leading the venture could have aligned interests include wanting to:

- Disrupt the market and being passionate about doing so
- Exploit a gap in the market
- Work with like-minded people
- Enjoy the challenge and buzz of a new a venture
- Make a difference to their existing business and its customers
- Earn a large financial pay-out from a successful startup

No matter what the interest is, the wise leader ensures there is interest alignment. The first step to ensuring interest alignment is to ensure there is no conflict of interest. It sounds obvious, but amazes me how many times both startups and ventures within corporations get this so badly wrong.

In a recent digital transformation project within a large UK retailer, the program lead hired several technology contractors to staff the program quickly and get going. Most of these contractors were motivated by their high day-rated salaries, paying a lower tax as a contractor, versus having to pay higher taxes as an employee and keeping their contract going for as long as possible. Hence, there was little interest in delivering solutions quickly or taking tough decisions when they faced them. Almost from the onset there was conflict of interest. While the program lead had other reasons for his use of contractors, the conflict of interest derailed his project.

Ensuring there is no conflict of interest is more of a science, whereas aligning interest is an art that the leader can learn and perfect. In my view, if you have ensured that there are no conflicts of interest, you are already set up to succeed with your team. However, if you can align interest from the onset, you will have a winning team capable of greatness.

Contrary to popular belief, those who drive an entrepreneurial venture forward are not primarily motivated by financial rewards alone. While financial rewards in terms of stock options and equity in the venture align interest for the long term, those are secondary.

It is the drive to prove a point, turn an idea into reality, and have fun that is far more important to those who are really succeeding. If someone is telling you during an interview that they are driven by the stock options your startup is providing, you have got the wrong person and can cut the interview short straight away. The money follows the idea and execution. It is a by-product and not the goal.

I was associated with a London-based startup in the digital product design space. They help their mainly corporate customers and startup clients work through nascent ideas and convert them into prototypes and products. The two co-founders were from a web agency background and had worked with some of the biggest London agencies in their sector. They intimately understood what these agencies were doing wrong, which led to their employees producing less than exciting work that ultimately disappointed their customers. The co-founders were determined to change this and prove the point that they could do this better than the big agencies. The result was their venture. They hired people with the right skills and freed them to express their talent. Working in small mission-focused teams in short assignments, they carefully selected talent who enjoyed that kind of work. Fast forward a few years and this two-man startup is a 100-plus strong agency with Fortune 500 clients from across the globe. The agency has recently been acquired by a large, publicly listed IT services firm.

Aligning interests with your team and venture can be extremely powerful and can unleash the enormous latent potential of your team.

Customer Centricity

If the people you are attracting cannot understand the need to think from the customer perspective, you have got a serious problem. They may not all understand this from day one, but if they cannot get around to the idea that your entire venture exists to solve a customer problem, it is unlikely they will add value.

Over time, the purpose of business has been distorted to be about sales, profits, and valuations. Few talk about the usefulness of the business to its customers and community. If the business cannot solve a customer problem and delight them in the process, the business is unlikely to have the time to worry about sales, profits, or any other financial metric. Delight customers or perish. The consumer has more choices than ever, due to their smartphone and the digital revolution. Your competitor is only a tap away.

If the team you are forming doesn't get this obsession for customer centricity, then you need a new team. They may not all get it at the onset, but if you emphasize the importance of the customer in all decision-making and activities, they should start to understand and act. This must be reflected in all initiatives and activities. This is why this book has been organized in the way it has been, to focus on the customer mission and journey first and how you are differentiating to deliver that delightful experience.

It would help to review the customer journey map developed as part of your strategy. Do this with your team, not in isolation, and do it often to ensure you stay relevant. This helps to keep the customer focus, stimulate fresh ideas, and validate learnings.

Living Agile

Up to the mid-1990s and just before the internet revolution, large businesses were mostly stable entities with steady growth. Five-year planning cycles and strategies still worked. The internet changed all of that almost overnight. The information and choice that became available to consumers posed a serious threat to opaque, rent seeking business models. If the internet created unlimited choice for consumers, the proliferation of the smartphone cemented the rise of the internet and created completely new digital-based business models, totally unimaginable before. The one thing unanimously agreed on is that this digital revolution has increased both the degree of change and pace of change for all businesses like never before.

Moreover, digital has fundamentally altered the economics of business. Prior to the internet, customers had to choose between high price, wide choice, great service, and cheap, limited choice, no-frills alternatives. Today they can have unlimited choice and great service at competitive prices. Think Amazon.

Additionally, first movers and winners take all in the digital economy. The rest are left to pick up the scraps or face extinction. Think of Netflix obliterating Blockbuster.

The implication of this is that if incumbents are to have any chance of surviving amidst all this digital disruption, they need to embrace agility. This gives them the best chance of repurposing their entire business to remain relevant. Agility allows them to achieve two things. Firstly, it gives the teams within the business the capability to adopt a test-learn, fail-fast, or scale approach. This helps them repurpose their business and remain relevant. However, this merely ensures protecting current revenues and doing better than existing competition, it doesn't guarantee survival against the disruptors. Secondly, the same agility can be leveraged to spin off arms-length initiatives to disrupt the disruptors. When incumbents roll out disruptive services, that is when the market takes notice and adoption crosses critical mass. The disruptive service is then mainstream.

So how do you and your teams live agile?

The Basics of Agile

Agile is in fashion at the time of writing and it is a good thing. Timeless values always get spun off as the new great thing, while if you looked slightly deeper you could understand agile as an organizational quality that has always been around a long while and has been adopted by successful organizations since the dawn of collective effort.

As often happens, agility is now touted as the latest and greatest management technique by expensive management consultants. Is it?

Agility isn't a management technique; it is the way an organization behaves. Agility isn't a process to get things done; rather, agility is an organizational quality to react rapidly and continuously improve as a team. Kanban, which has now been made famous by popular kanban board tools such as Jira and Trello, is a visual tool that is underpinned by transparency and agility.

Agile Teams

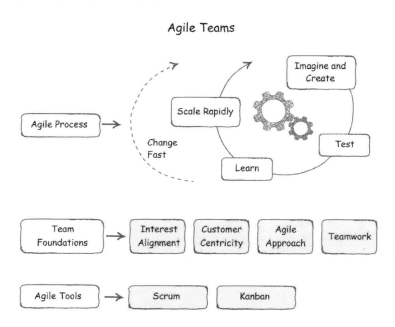

One of my biggest blessings in life is to have worked for Toyota. As part of a major IT upgrade for their Vietnam operations, I was involved in an intense all-consuming project for six months. The project touched every aspect of Toyota's operations.

It is widely acknowledged that Toyota founded lean manufacturing. What we today recognize as the 'agile method' is essentially the lean manufacturing approach applied to non-manufacturing businesses.

My first-hand experience at Toyota helped me understand the essence of the agile method and what really works and what doesn't. Agile is made up of logical steps:

Imagine / Create

Creation is the essence of value creation. Be it the final product or an intermediate product, such as a blueprint, unless you bring something into existence, you cannot get interest or feedback.

Test

Test your product with actual users and get feedback and observe the product in usage.

Technology Tools

Observe and learn based on actual usage. Not what you imagine to be happening, but what is actually happening.

Scale Rapidly (or Change Fast)

Once you have a product that delights its target customers and they would be willing to pay for it, you need to scale it up rapidly using the teams discussed earlier. The reason is that competition latches on quickly and the speed is key to incrementally capture tacit knowledge derived from serving increasingly larger users. This tacit knowledge creates an invisible but formidable barrier to entry for the copycats.

Agile Tools – Scrums

One of perhaps the most popular of agile methods today, Scrum is a project management approach that encourages teams to self-organize and deliver functionality iteratively in short cycles called sprints (one or two weeks long). One of the Scrum rituals is to do a daily stand-up meeting lasting no more than 15 minutes, where each member of the team answers three simple questions:

1. What have I done since we last met?
2. What am I doing now?
3. What are the blockers, if any, to doing what I need to do?

The objective of the sprint is to deliver a working product (or part of a product) to a customer to get feedback. This creates the short development cycles focused on creating value and minimizing value.

The simple Scrum ritual can be very powerful in bonding teams and getting great things done.

Agile Tools – Kanban

One of the tools used together with Scrum is kanban. It is a simple, visual way of identifying what work needs to be done, i.e. 'to-do', what is 'in-progress' and what is 'done'.

The to-do list is a list of features derived from original design and customer feedback to previous releases. It is also known as the product backlog. The team essentially works during each sprint to move as many items within the to-do list to the done list, and in the process agree which features add the most value to the customer.

Embracing and living the agile approach brings together teams in ways that are quite amazing. The output from an agile team can be exponentially greater than a siloed approach. An agile organization becomes and behaves like a nimble organism that adapts quickly, survives, and thrives.

Embrace Uncertainty but Stay Focused

By its very nature, any new venture faces uncertainty. In the competitive business world, if you are a startup you face extreme uncertainty in terms of product market fit, scaling challenges, and attracting and retaining the right talent. Failure means dashed dreams and possible significant financial pain. If you are starting a new initiative within a corporation, in addition to the risks faced by the startup, additional risks exist around managing stakeholders, deadlines, and the political ramifications associated with any breakaway success. Hence, both the entrepreneur and the intrapreneur face extreme uncertainty.

Such levels of pressure are often enough to unnerve many and derail their whole venture. However, those who are successful embrace the wisdom of uncertainty. They understand that they and their team can respond to any challenges that come their way. In fact, they anticipate and welcome challenges because they understand that if they are not encountering challenges as they grow their ventures, they are probably not doing something worthwhile. This behavior is vital for the team to succeed because a leader needs to create a safe operating environment for the team even while they faces uncertainty.

Not everyone in the team is an entrepreneurial risk taker who wants to change the world. Many in the team are skilled specialists who just want to do a great job, feel satisfied, and take home a paycheck. These team members need to feel secure in order to perform at their best. Imagine a leader who constantly worries the team about the uncertainties. The team would soon be worrying too much instead of delivering, and would soon leave. This doesn't mean that the team is insulated from customers or the market. On the contrary, they should be actively engaging with the customers and benchmarking against competition directly. After all, a business that succeeds in a competitive marketplace is simply a better team than the other teams that play in that same space.

Put Results Before Process

Regardless of the stage the team is at, it needs to focus on results. Results, not processes, deliver value to customers. The customer doesn't care what happens behind the scenes. However, if you have broken processes behind the scenes, the customer will eventually feel it in terms of degraded service. Process needs to be continuously improved, but the goal here isn't to improve the process but the customer experience.

Startup Teams

The Visionary Leader and Driver

Are great teams formed or do they come together naturally? Businesspeople often talk about forming great teams. In my observation, the reality is slightly different. Successful teams and businesses seem, perhaps counterintuitively, to come together naturally. I witnessed this first-hand at Homegrown, my property crowdfunding startup. The CEO did a great job of communicating the vision of the business, which allowed him to raise early-stage seed capital. As soon as this was picked up by the startup media we started to be approached by talented people who wanted to join the team. The caliber and pedigree of some of these people took me by surprise. This was in stark contrast to my previous experience. Before Homegrown, in a large corporation where I headed up the digital transformation, we faced enormous challenges in attracting talent.

I vividly remember a conversation with a high-flying technology consultant from one of the Big Four technology consultancies. He was pitching to join the business. I asked him whether he was fully aware of the risks of throwing away a career in a large corporation in exchange for a startup that had just received funding at the seed stage. He convinced me that the vision, the founding team, and the opportunity to make an early impact in an industry was driving his decision. He was aware of the risks of joining a startup but had calculated that the experience gained would only add to his illustrious career. It was difficult to argue with that one.

Clarity bestows confidence, which then attracts opportunities in terms of capital and talent. This is why I've emphasized reaching clarity on both the business and personal fronts. Through the tools explored in the earlier chapters, the leader should be able to reach clarity on how to enhance the customer journey profitably. This clarity then allows the leader to communicate a compelling vision and strategy to attract the capital and talent required to make that come true. The law of attraction seems to be in play. This has been my first-hand experience in the startups as well as in corporations.

We have all seen how charismatic leaders can make a huge difference to businesses. However, not all of us are endowed with charisma. I'm a firm believer that if you are clear in your vision and define a bold strategy, you will attract like-minded people to join your team and help you. If clarity bestows confidence, then confidence seems to bestow charisma.

So, I created the tools that are presented in this book to allow you to reach that clarity.

If you have created the right vision and strategy and are able to communicate that clearly, by using some of the tools shared with you earlier, you will face a different dilemma. You will probably be attracting a lot of people who want to join your venture. How do you then hire the right talent?

The first three hires in a new team, in addition to the main founder, are vital to the success of the venture. These four people will set the benchmark, culture, and tone for the organization for years to come. This happens quite naturally. Even though the founding team may not be consciously setting these standards during recruitment, they subconsciously filter people of standards similar to themselves. It is vital you get the hiring right from the onset. In the ensuing sections I share how.

Hire for Deep Innovation and Domain Secrets

When venture capitalists fund teams they look for a few things to predict success. What are the key predictors of success? One is experience in the founding team. If the team is attempting to disrupt an industry, it helps enormously if at least a few members have deep insider information about that particular industry. For example, it would be odd for a group of people to make a huge impact within the finance industry if none of them have a financial background.

Venture capitalists are looking for what they call 'domain secrets'. Only when you have spent sufficient time deep within an industry, will you be able to understand the inner workings, both the obvious and the hidden. You will also have grasped the exact levers that make a difference, what is really useful, and what is a waste. Many of the successful fintech inventions we see today, such as crowdfunding or low-cost international money transfer, result from industry insiders understanding what waste they can eliminate in the customer journey, and what aspects they can speed up or simplify, reducing cost and enhancing the experience at the same time.

In hiring teams, I look for domain experts who have already made improvements or innovations in their respective fields. This is important, because in a startup you will need to continuously improve the product offer and be receptive to rapid change.

However, deep expertise should not be confused with an illustrious CV. Having progressed in a corporate career isn't an indication of success. Someone who navigated the politics of an organization and was promoted may not bring the hard skills you need to develop your product. You need builders not talkers. Yet so many startups fall into this trap of thinking that a high-flyer from an industry big name will add kudos to their startup.

It would be unrealistic to expect that all the skills required are already present when you form the team. It is more practical to find a team that has the foundational skills and domain knowledge already, but is curious and willing to learn new ideas and concepts, and adapt them for the product they are delivering.

Swiss Army Knives

During the startup phase, the team will need to juggle numerous activities. Unlike a large business, which would have a separate function for operations, finance, technology, human resources, and so on, a startup would have to do all of this, but it is spread across a small team.

We would need team members whose main role would be to develop and test a product with customers. These members then need to pick up the additional tasks to keep the venture going. This is where we need people with the Swiss Army knife mindset, who are adept at doing the various tasks as required, and not boxing themselves into a specific title or role.

Soft Skills and Team Dynamics

In sports, as in business, there is a strange phenomenon. One would believe that if you formed teams comprising of superstars, logic dictates that it should be the winning team. However, we know this isn't true. Repeatedly, both sports teams and businesses have tried to form teams full of superstars but have ended up failing quite miserably.

Long-Term Capital Management is a good example. It was a massive hedge fund with US$126 billion under management at one point. However, it almost collapsed. Just prior to this it had focused on quantitative stock trading, which involves automated high-speed trading using mathematical formulas. To achieve this, it hired top mathematicians and scientists from NASA, who were the best and brightest in the mathematical field. Logic dictates that these experts should have had no trouble in mastering the mathematics of the stock market. Yet they still got it so badly wrong that Long-Term Capital Management nearly went under. History is ridden with similar examples in all areas of sports, business, and government, where people have naively attempted to build a high-performing team filled with superstars. It doesn't work, and simple observation explains why.

High-performing teams consist of members who are all playing their best game. Importantly, they bring unique skills to the team and exchange these skills freely and transparently with the other members of the team. In such cases the team performance is far greater than that of any one individual member. Members of the team are not burdened by superstar egos, which prevents unproductive competition within the team.

So, do such teams form by themselves or is there some science behind this? In my view you can shape the team with proven methodology.

Tools such as personality type testing can make a positive difference to the team composition. Taking the time to allow the team to discover the personalities of their various members can be valuable throughout the business. Helping the team go through this exercise together allows them to discover that different people think differently and approach the same situation from alternative angles. This increases trust and tolerance, and reduces friction. Take for example a highly introverted engineer who prefers not to plan but to get straight into writing great software. Knowing this preferred style of working early allows others to not expect too much banter with this person or for them to be very involved in planning.

Personality tests are becoming ever more accessible and some good ones are even free. Investing the time to do this as a group can prevent so much headache for the team and its leader throughout their journey. Links to free online personality tests can be found in the Resources section at the end of this chapter.

My own experience of doing this with the team created a level of trust very quickly, as people appreciated that everyone in the team thinks differently. The team started becoming more productive faster and, importantly, was having fun in the process. Enjoying the process is far more energizing then stewing in self-made assumptions. I cannot recommend this process highly enough if you are forming a team. As soon as you have a few members in the team, get them to do a personality-type test, and talk about how they will use the results to communicate better as a team, including what they will do and what they will stop doing.

In addition, as a leader you need to be cognizant of the composition of the team. If you are forming a product engineering team, on the surface it may appear that those who bring new ideas to solve the problem would be valuable to the team. Unconsciously you may end up hiring people into the team who are all idea innovators. This is a recipe for disaster. You will soon find that the entire team is coming up with ideas, but few are being implemented, and people spend more time defending their idea, rather than making it happen and testing it with the real customers.

There are tools such as Belbin team roles that help identify what roles people enjoy doing within teams. Some people enjoy creating ideas, while others enjoy coordinating different team members. Some enjoy investigating various options, while others enjoy implementing them. The Belbin tool can help team members to discover their preferences and, when shared with the team, it can help bring out the best in individuals and the team. Please refer to the Resources section for a link to the Belbin tool.

Understanding the disposition of each team member helps to form a balanced team. Importantly, this knowledge can ensure the person is in the role that is compatible with their nature and what the business needs to achieve. In practical terms, it is almost impossible to construct a team that is functionally high skilled and whose personalities and natures complement each other. However, understanding how people actually work and their preferences will ensure that you don't try to fit a square peg in a round hole.

This can be enormously valuable, because it prevents or minimizes friction within the team and makes it more productive. Trying to fix members who are holding the team behind can be overwhelming for many entrepreneurs and can derail them completely. Preventing this early can set up your team to succeed.

I've also observed another key contributor to the formation of high-performing, successful teams. Invariably, many of these teams have common backgrounds. A business I worked with, which has grown to US$1 billion in revenue within 15 years, had founders who came from the same previous employer. They left an IT services company as a group and set up on their own. The venture eventually grew to be a very successful global business with over 25,000 employees.

Similarly, the founders of a startup in London, which has radically changed the business finance space, came from Oxford University.

In my view, the core team of a startup ideally should have a common background and some shared history. This creates a strong bond within the team, which allows them to come together to overcome the numerous challenges that the startup will face.

At the risk of sounding politically incorrect, the common background and shared history of the team trumps diversity as a predictor of success, in my view. I'm not advocating uniform thinking here, more that people who have worked together before and succeeded together intuitively understand the team dynamics. It may well be that they are from a particular background, but what matters is that they are individually skilled and work well as a team.

A recent management fad states that if you attract a very diverse team, you will outperform a more homogeneous team. While I'm all for diversity and true inclusion, in a startup environment this isn't the highest priority. While diversity brings new ideas and challenges old status quos, this is less relevant to a startup. A successful startup isn't about the number of ideas but the brilliant execution of a few. Diversity helps to shake things up in an old, staid organization and can catalyze change. That isn't where startup businesses find themselves. Hire based on merit and fit, and more likely than not you will end up with a diverse, thriving team anyway.

Hire People Who Can Grow with the Business

Not having the right team is one of the top reasons cited by startup founders for the cause of their failure. However, when I probe further, many of them confess that they did start with a great team, but the team and the business lost its way after some time. This is a thinking error in my view. There is no such thing as a great team that lasts forever. No soccer team repeatedly wins the championship every year. However, there are soccer clubs that form great teams every year and do well in the championships repeatedly. In his memoirs, the legendary Manchester United team manager, Sir Alex Ferguson, talks about how he continuously shaped a team every year, letting go of players who had become less relevant and attracting new talent. Yet there have been players who stayed with the team for many years, remaining highly productive and valuable. They did this by adapting with the team as it changed and grew.

The same logic applies in business. Inevitably, growth brings change to the business. A five-man startup is a very different beast to a 50-person organization that is growing rapidly, and again that is very different to a 500-person organization. Successful contributors change and adapt as the organization grows. If they don't, and stick to what they did previously, this often leads to friction, not just with other members of the team, but with customers also. Founders get blindsided by this, thinking those who started with them in their garage are also the right people to run the organization when it is growing rapidly. Often, it isn't the case.

When founding teams are able to change rapidly it becomes a huge advantage, because the team retains tacit knowledge. They know their operations and customers inside out. A growth mindset and embracing change is key to succeeding here. Founding teams that can continuously keep up with rapid growth, changing customers' expectations, and market demands become increasingly valuable over time.

Align to Strategy

Now that you have formed a high-performing team, one of your biggest challenges will be to get the team to pull together in the same direction, even through challenging times. This is where an agile digital strategy blueprint can align your team. The blueprint, when created and reviewed together as a team, can become a focal point for the organization—your team's guiding North Star.

I highly encourage you to involve the team in the strategy creation process. Even if you have conceived of the idea and done much of the strategy creation on your own, it always helps to share with your team and ask them to take it to the next level. Undoubtedly, the team will create a better version of your strategy, and most importantly they will buy into your vision and strategy. This, as we've already seen, is priceless. The simple act of spending a few hours with a team to create the strategy and then to involve them continually in the refinement of the strategy based on customer feedback, can prove to be the number one factor in keeping your team aligned, energized, and productive.

Empower and Enjoy

As the founder driving the vision and strategy, you will be tempted to have your hands in all parts of the business and to share in every decision. Please resist. You probably cannot do more damage than when trying to micromanage a high-performing team. Great leaders hire people who are better than they are, yet are able to win the respect and admiration of their teams to achieve the seemingly impossible. On the other hand, I've yet to meet a highly successful micromanager. The truth is blatantly obvious. If you trust and empower your team to deliver the best, while coaching and keeping them motivated, you are more likely to achieve far greater results than if you micromanage them.

It is not natural for us to let go of things, especially things we care about deeply. This is where we need to find a balance between what is right for the customers we are creating for, and what is right for us personally. By allowing the team to make good decisions and not penalizing failure, you will empower them to experiment and create the right product for the customers. Yet you as the leader should play an important role, where you challenge the team with high expectations; it is unlikely you will succeed by releasing yet one more mediocre product into an already overcrowded marketplace. Set high expectations that challenge the team, but resist being the know-it-all who insists on having all the solutions. I've never come across a more disempowering behavior.

Corporate Digital Transformation and New Venture Teams

The Digital Transformation Dilemma

Digital transformation initiatives are challenging. Only three out of ten initiatives achieve anything near their original objectives. Yet every major company has some sort of a digital transformation plan as part of its five-year strategy. It is almost taboo not to have a digital transformation plan as part of any decent strategy. The rise of digital disruptors in every industry, including retail, transport, travel, and finance, means incumbents face enormous pressure to counter the disruptors with their own digital solutions.

Uber has disrupted several taxi companies without owning any taxis. Airbnb has disrupted the hotel industry without owning any rooms. Amazon has permanently changed the retail landscape without owning any stores. Moreover, digital disruptors corner the vast majority of an industry, leaving very little for the other players. This threatens the very existence of the incumbents, who have built up a business over many decades and cannot change rapidly.

This puts the pressure on incumbents to create a bold digital strategy or react to a disturbance in the industry from digital disruptors. This often means a transformation of the entire business model. However, very often incumbents see digital transformation as simply adding a few websites or apps to existing business models.

In reality, radical transformation doesn't sit well with stakeholders, paid employees, executives, or shareholders. So, companies often end up making severe compromises in terms of their transformation, delivering a few technological enhancements, but don't offer anything radically different.

Consider online flight ticket comparison websites such as Skyscanner. They disrupted the flight booking industry by providing a comparison of prices across several airlines. To counter the threat posed by such price transparency, most airlines reacted by building their own websites, which allowed customers to book their own tickets online. Airlines understood that customers wanted price comparison; however, providing price comparison would damage their business model. Skyscanner is a true digital disruption, whereas the airline websites made only minor, cosmetic upgrades.

Yet so many organizations undertake such cosmetic upgrades in the name of digital transformation, aiming to make an impact on the disruptors. The team in charge of delivering such an ambitious goal often ends up failing. One of the aims of this book is to give managers an agile digital strategy blueprint, so that they can help shape the solution and understand the entire process from strategy to execution.

Ministry of Transformation? (Common Blunders)

A Real-Life Example

A CEO notices that sales within his group of B2B industrial businesses have been below the market rate of growth for several years. Despite a concerted effort by his team to bring sales and margins in line with the market, these efforts are failing. He believes that while small, digital disruptors in his industry are a threat, they are niche players targeting very specific product categories, unlike his group businesses, which distribute almost every manufacturer's product in his industry. He doesn't see these small players as a credible threat, or if they emerge as one he is confident that he will be able to acquire and integrate them within his group. Nevertheless, he and his board remain concerned that, over time, these small digital disruptors, if left unchecked, could pose a serious threat.

As part of his five-year strategy, he prioritizes digital and instructs his top team that digital transformation of the business is high on the agenda. After some planning, his top team agrees that a digital transformation function needs to be set up and resourced. In due course, a Chief Digital Transformation Officer (CDTO) is hired and mandated to lead the business's digital transformation efforts. As part of their job, they must detract from the digital disruptors and ensure that the organization is suitably transformed to thrive in the digital age.

The CDTO sets about their job with much enthusiasm and support from the rest of the organization during several whiteboarding and brainstorming sessions to formulate the digital transformation strategy. To everyone's shock, that strategy involves reorganizing the entire business, breaking down existing functions, and forming customer-oriented product teams. The enthusiasm soon diminishes when people realize that old structures and ways of doing things within the organization are all at risk. The once enthusiastic department leaders are now quietly opposing and undermining the CDTO's plans. The CEO has to step in to arbitrate, but then realizes the bad will stems from risking current sales for something potentially beneficial that may arise if the transformation goes ahead.

Fast forward two years and the CDTO is no longer with the business. Interestingly, they have moved on to yet another transformation role in another similar business.

For the B2B industrial distributor, although it still remains a large player, the growth has stalled.

While the above is a real-life example, we could have picked an example like this from almost any industry. Knee-jerk reactions and trying to respond to digital disruption using the same management approach of creating yet another department, don't produce results. Moreover, when vested interests within existing organizations have to be challenged in order to make any real transformation, the status quo almost always wins out.

The current management structures of siloed departments, each specializing in their own areas, are a product of the industrial age. It mirrors the factory lines that Henry Ford set up, where each worker focused on a specific task and didn't need to interact with any other workers. This was super-efficient when producing goods in a factory line; however, in the digital age, where almost every function in a business needs to cooperate in order to deliver an excellent customer experience, this siloed approach doesn't work. Yet we see organization after organization throw the same old management structures at a completely new problem like digital disruption. A few organizations, however, are taking good advantage of innovative ways of working and reaping its benefits.

Digital Garages

Wise C-level leaders of these large corporations have begun to understand that cosmetic fixes don't work. The million-dollar consultants and the fact-finding, first-class trips to Silicon Valley have helped open the eyes of many boards. They now begin to understand the severity of the threat posed by digital disruptors and have witnessed the collapse of giants such as Nokia, Blockbuster, and Sears. They have also seen millions wasted in cosmetic transformations that fail to win back customers or restore profits.

Companies who are determined to thrive in the digital era have asked hard questions of themselves. Why are their well-funded digital teams failing to deliver? Why are their teams demoralized, repeatedly failing, and even disappearing?

I once met a wise senior executive, nearing retirement, of a 200,000-person global business. He was refreshingly open and spoke of things as they were. Over a dinner, we were pondering why digital transformation teams fail so often and so badly. He summed it up using a beautiful analogy.

"If you had showed the first car ever made to the horseman, he would have convinced you why a better horse carriage was the future," he said with perfect conviction.

Yet with every digital transformation, the teams involved are doing exactly that: showing shiny new cars to people used to horse carriages. The inertia of staying with the horse carriage cannot be underestimated. The other problem is what do we do with our horses? How dare you suggest that we put them down when they have worked so well for us?

A well-known UK retailer I've worked with found itself in this same situation. They had tried repeated digital transformation initiatives and ended up with a demoralized team and board. They decided to try something else. What if they moved those trying to make new cars away from the horseman? Then the car makers need not convince the horseman just because they were working for the same organization. Convincing those who may have little impact was a pointless exercise to begin with anyway.

So, they setup a digital garage in London, away from their headquarters, and hired a team that looked very different from their previous IT teams. The team was given high-level objectives on the business strategy and the problems they needed to solve. At the same time, business subject matter experts (SMEs) with deep operating experience within the chain retailer were embedded in these new tech teams to help share customer or colleague pain points. These business SMEs were specifically told not to talk about solution constraints; that was the role of the tech team, which had autonomy to deliver the solution in a manner it saw fit.

This act of top-level sponsorship, separation, high level objectives, and autonomy has started to bear fruit for this retailer. Its London-based tech teams are starting to come up with solutions to long-standing problems, such as excess inventory, slow product changeovers at stores, and many more issues once thought impossible to fix. The benefits are accruing for this business. This R&D lab approach with autonomy is delivering real benefits and catalyzing the traditional parts of the organization to change.

Interestingly, the teams in its new London digital garage are sought after by the rest of the business to create solutions for their own functions. It is also driving talented people within the retailer to join these now prestigious tech teams. The teams are regarded as problem-solvers and solution creators. Rebels within the business with ideas are now welcome within these teams, and these once-misfits are starting to thrive when they see their long-held ideas take shape.

The fact that existing employees can also upskill themselves by becoming part of these tech teams has helped numerous employees with deep domain expertise to stay with the business and add value.

Forming digital transformation teams within an existing large corporation needs some fresh, bold thinking, as demonstrated by the case of the retailer. The top-down siloed model of traditional organizations doesn't lend itself well to countering or creating digital disruption. However, by creating independent, satellite, well-funded teams, the benefits can be enormous.

Funding Teams, Not Projects

The more forward-thinking organizations handling digital transformation well understand that they need to act more like venture capitalists. Venture capitalists do not fund projects, they fund teams. They recognize that talented teams create great products that customers love and will pay for. They also recognize that such great products are not created out of a well-defined project, which starts and ends at specified times. In fact, trying to develop a product under project conditions creates the wrong kind of behaviors, where the team ends up with time pressure, so compromises on the product, which then flops with customers. Rather, venture capitalists understand that products are iterated on over time. Releasing quickly to customers, getting real feedback, and iterating to the next version in fixed, fast feedback cycles is key to getting to product market fit.

The additional benefit of funding teams and not projects is that teams learn and grow while projects succeed or fail. While a team may not develop a profitable product, it will always learn on the journey. This learning is valuable and can be reapplied as part of another initiative.

Finally, funding teams forces them to work with a limited budget and become resourceful. It cuts waste.

While the funding of teams idea is gaining traction as it increases the odds of success, it only works if you are funding the right teams. Just like venture capitalists, who vet hundreds of teams before they fund a few, you need to ensure that the right team is in place. However, if you are forming these teams, you have the benefit of ensuring they meet the independent unit test.

Independent Units

Unlike the startup, where the core team formation is less deliberate, one has to be more careful in setting up a transformation team. In a corporate context, the team is unlikely to have the same degree of freedom to create. Hence, it is paramount that certain factors are set in place from the onset.

Authority to Proceed

The team must have the authority to work on the project or venture. Usually, a high-profile sponsor, which has the CEO taking a direct interest, helps firstly to get the rest of the organization out of the way, and possibly then to start helping this team. Which self-respecting corporate employee doesn't want to be involved in the CEO's project?

Funded Teams

Ensure that the team has its own approved budget from the onset, and freedom to use the budget as the team sees fit, without the need for further approvals. The last thing you want is for the effort to be derailed by budget approval and payment bureaucracy.

Small / Fully Skilled

You want to make sure that each team is small. No more than six or seven people per team. Amazon has a famous rule: each team can be fed with just two pizzas.

At the same time, the team must have all the skill sets required to deliver the product. As a rule, the team shouldn't be looking outside to get things done. It can look for information, but it is responsible for building the product and delivering it.

Conventionally, companies tend to put their functional experts rather than multiskilled personnel on such teams. As an example, if finance, design, user experience, and software engineering skills are required to deliver the product, then conventionally you had people joining from these departments. Recipe for disaster. Departments and titles do not confer skills. Rather, it is better to skew the team towards people who actually build, and get the other skills multitasked by one or a few individuals.

Accountable End to End

The team must be accountable from inception to delivery, and for the product's scalability. The team should conceive, build, test, and scale the product. When this is clear to both team members and external stakeholders, the team is more likely to focus on value-adding activities. Giving the team this end-to-end responsibility is also empowering. When the team can make its own decisions without external interference, it focuses minds on making the right decisions and taking responsibility for those decisions.

Teams at startup stage focus on getting to product market fit. Success for these teams means getting to a viable product ready for growth. This is when smart organizations configure their teams for the next growth-oriented phase.

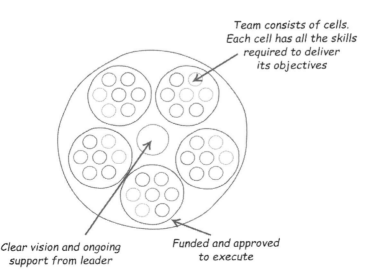

Team consists of cells. Each cell has all the skills required to deliver its objectives

Clear vision and ongoing support from leader

Funded and approved to execute

Teams for Scale-Ups

Put Growth Before Product

Once your venture has found its product market fit, your business will be entering the scale-up stage. You and your team will be in new territory and will face a different set of challenges, those associated with growth.

Whether you started as an entrepreneur-driven startup or within a corporate venture, the team challenges associated with the scale up-stage are common to both.

At the startup stage, the problem your team was solving was to find a fit between a customer need and your new digital product. Now that you have solved that, the scale-up stage is about getting the growth process right. Going from 100 satisfied customers to 1,000 needs a different mindset and understanding.

In the startup phase, the focus is on the product. In the scale-up phase it is about getting various processes right to be able to handle volumes. The first 100 customers could have become raving fans of yours. It is easy to think that the superiority of your product caused them to become raving fans. In reality you are more likely to have solved a common problem for these early adopters.

As you go from 100 to the first 1,000, the second 100 may still like your product but they have a slightly different problem. Hence, you may need to add more features to satisfy these incremental custom-ers. This is where the product mindset of ever-increasing innovations to satisfy customers starts to harm the business. The more profitable thing to do is find another 100 customers who value the product with only minor variations. This keeps the core of the product stable and keeps intact the value created for customers, while being just dynamic enough to vary features to attract the next incremental customer base.

The team needs to move from pure product development to busi-ness development at this stage. Good old revenue and profits take in-creasing priority, and driving the numbers should become fashionable at this stage. While it is simple to say this, the team may not intui-tively recognize this, especially when it has been successful in product development.

In addition, the natural inclination and interests of a team involved in product development is different from one flogging the engine of sales growth. Many startups and ventures fail at this juncture. They cannot pivot from product to the growth process.

While possibly painful, some rationalization and reorganization of the team may be required to make this transition. This isn't about morphing the business into traditional siloed functions such as sales, operations, and finance. Rather, self-contained teams are still held in place, but the composition of the team is slanted more towards people who drive growth rather than engineers who keep improving the products.

Sustained Managerial Intensity

Reconstituting the teams provides new direction; direction that is geared for growth. However, direction is pointless without momentum, and to create momentum you need managerial intensity to provide the energy to keep growing the business. Here I focus on managerial intensity rather than leadership of the founder because each team needs its own manager who helps drive the objectives. The leader now has to take the role of leading these managers as opposed to the whole founding team.

Such managerial intensity is different from the entrepreneurial drive of a founder. It is more sustained. It is the ability to repeat fairly boring activities with some enthusiasm while striving for improvements. While the growth phase provides the excitement of revenue, valuation, and team growth, underpinning the growth is often a routine to make it happen. Hence, the managerial intensity needs to be sustained over time.

Now You Need the Foxes

Political astuteness of the leader and manager plays a key role in the growth phase. While politics is a dirty word within the startup environment, it is simply a description of how people behave when put into groups. In very small teams, negative politics can be minimized, but as the teams grow and the number of teams within the business grows, politics can only be managed and not avoided. This is where the team needs managers and leaders with political savvy, to increase the team's effectiveness and keep its communications flowing at the right levels.

Playing a Team Game

During my secondary school years in Singapore, I had the opportunity to try out many sports. The school had a big rugby culture, though it wasn't one of my favorites. Badminton was more my game, and I was putting in a lot of effort to make it onto the school team and play at the national level. One day, during a grueling badminton training session with a teammate, unknown to me, the headmaster of the school, Mr. Eugene Wijeysingha, was standing by the court watching us play. When the match finished, I greeted the headmaster, and in response he said, "Have you considered playing rugby? You would do well for your height."

It was quite clear what the instruction was, and the following week I found myself training with the school rugby team. I came to enjoy the sport, as it was quite liberating and, importantly, a team sport. You cannot win alone in rugby.

As we were all looking forward to the school holidays, the rugby coach had an announcement. We had to come back for three straight days during the holiday for a 'bonus' training session. A few players from the New Zealand All Blacks team were coming to train us, and we were expected to be at the training session for three days from 7 a.m. to 7 p.m.

Even as 15-year-olds, we knew what a big deal the New Zealand All Blacks were and what a privilege it was to be trained by their players. The training took place at the Padang, which is the national field overlooked by impressive, colonial government buildings and sixty-story skyscrapers—a truly magnificent sight etched in my memory.

I went for the training and came out permanently changed. Those were the three most life-changing days of my life, where I realized so many things. I saw how grown boys can be driven to tears when physically and mentally stretched. But, the human body is amazingly capable, and one's physical endurance can be stretched beyond one's wildest imagination.

I saw how the All Blacks players, towering giants and masters at their game, could casually walk around, seemingly without care, be aware of everything that was happening on the field, but be oblivious to everything just outside the perimeter of play. At the end of those three days my team's game was permanently changed and we were playing several notches higher. The ball was magically flowing amongst a team that was charging forward at speeds not known to us before. It seemed like magic, as suddenly there would be the right person in the right place to receive the ball and press forward to the try line.

It took me many years as a technologist, business strategist, and yoga practitioner to comprehend what happened during those three days with the New Zealand All Blacks.

Several times during each day of the training we practiced the 'Haka', which is a ceremonial, Maori dance performed by the All Blacks before each game. The team does a synchronous, loud chanting in Maori, with aggressive, dance-like moves. It is energizing just to watch. Whenever we practiced the Haka, we were uplifted as a team, but it took me a while to fully comprehend its effects.

One day, as I was doing my yoga practice and meditation, I realized the Haka is the equivalent of the invocation in yoga. In group yogic meditation our teacher always started with an invocation or chant, which the whole group did together. His explanation was that the chant brought together and aligned the energies of the individuals to a combined energy. That was really what was happening with the Haka. The team came together, not just physically and mentally, but at the energy level.

In the business context, I witnessed a similar phenomenon in both Japanese companies and Indian IT services. Japanese construction companies organized synchronous, light exercises at the start of each workday. Similarly, top Indian IT services companies organized yoga classes for its teams at the beginning of each day.

I encourage you to explore and find your team's Haka. When you bring together a team, not just physically and mentally, but at the energy level, you will become formidable, just like the New Zealand All Blacks.

Resources

Personality Test and Team Building Tools

The Myers-Briggs Type Indicator® (MBTI®) assessment was designed to help a person better understand what makes them tick, how they relate to others, and how they can benefit from this knowledge in everyday life. The self-awareness achieved through this test helps individuals understand how they function and, in turn, move into more fulfilling roles.

https://www.mbtionline.com

16Personalities offers a free personality test tool. The test can be taken quickly online.

https://www.16personalities.com/free-personality-test

While MBTI® and 16Personalities focus on an individual's drivers, Belbin's team roles focuses on what roles individuals play in a team. Understanding how people operate within teams can be useful to ensure you don't have the wrong person for the role.

https://www.belbin.com/resources/blogs/basic-steps-in-team-building/

Useful Books and Videos

Who is a guide to hiring top talent. Geoff Smart and Randy Street provide a simple and practical solution to a key problem any business faces—attracting top talent. Based on more than 1,300 hours of interviews with more than 20 billionaires and 300 CEOs, *Who* presents Smart and Street's 'A Method for Hiring'. Refined through the largest research study of its kind ever undertaken, the method stresses fundamental elements that anyone can implement.

Stanford University has produced a video in which Anu Hariharan, Partner at Y Combinator Continuity, speaks with Vinod Khosla, Founder of Khosla Ventures and former founding CEO and co-founder of Sun Microsystems, to learn about hiring mindsets.

https://www.youtube.com/watch?v=alqHBCkSN8I&feature=youtu.be

Agile Tools

Trello is a kanban board that helps teams to track work. It provides a visual way of tracking work and allows teams to collaborate from anywhere. Teams can organize work through a system of boards, lists, and cards.

Jira is another kanban board but has significantly more features than Trello and is oriented for software development projects. A neat feature of Jira is its ability to connect with other software development environments and continuous integration tools to manage the end-to-end process of software development.

Confluence is a modern approach for teams to manage work artefacts and communicate on projects, with a focus on lightweight documentation and collaboration. Decision and learning logs can help teams to focus on output rather than meetings and communications.

Slack is a messaging collaboration tool where you and your team can work together to get things done. When used well, you can get rid of emails using Slack. In Slack, work happens in channels, which can help manage several distinct pieces of work.

Great things in business are never done by one person. They're done by a team of people.

~ Steve Jobs ~

Chapter 6
Agile Technology

Next to people, the biggest reason cited by entrepreneurs for start-up failure is technology. When asked what went wrong with technology, sadly, many are unable to explain. That is because the real reason for failure isn't technology, but the entrepreneur not understanding it.

Frankly, I don't blame the entrepreneur at all. Digital technology that powers the internet has grown and evolved so rapidly since 1995 that it isn't surprising that anyone trying to make sense of it all would be overwhelmed.

I consider myself very fortunate that my career (as a self-taught, web software engineer in 1998) began around the time when the internet started to take off. Since then my career has evolved around internet-related technologies involving both large corporations and cutting-edge startups around the world.

I confess I found both the degree and rate of change around internet technologies overwhelming on many occasions. Fortunately, I worked out and refined a simple model to explain technology to those who didn't have a technical background, my teams, and even myself! I share this model with you here in this chapter. It is an essential part of the customer-centered agile digital strategy blueprint.

Before we explore the technology model, let's understand why the entrepreneur needs an excellent grasp of the technology powering their venture.

Kirsty, who we met earlier in the book, ran a venture that came up with a clever, digital solution to the key handover problem in Airbnb rentals. However, her chances of startup success were ruined when the people she had entrusted with technology development were not aligned to her vision, and not helped by her lack of understanding and general technophobia.

I've met many founders who were pulling their hair out because they didn't understand technology and, as a result, had major friction with their tech teams. Many of these founders had excellent domain knowledge and great soft skills. However, not understanding technology the right way handicapped them. The ever-increasing noise of yet another daily technology buzzword only weakened their confidence. Confusion leads to poor and often expensive decisions, which doomed the startups they worked so hard to build. This is such a waste.

The model I share here helps to simplify digital technology and gives entrepreneurs and their teams a common, authoritative vocabulary. This clarity helps cut out the noise, allowing them to focus on what matters.

Why Every Modern Entrepreneur Needs to Grasp Technology

There is one benefit to the fear of technology. It can be harnessed to ensure that you make the right decisions from the onset, because not doing so has proven catastrophic for many startups.

However, there are many upsides to understanding and leveraging the right technology. Technology is an enabler. It is a means to create a product that solves a customer problem in a delightful manner. Technology in itself isn't the solution. Some founders with deep technical knowledge create startups with all the latest technology. Their startup is peppered with artificial intelligence, machine learning, blockchain, and every new buzzword you can think of. Often theirs is a solution looking for a problem. From this perspective, not being a technology expert can be a blessing, as you would find the approach of my agile digital strategy blueprint natural to follow, starting with the industry and customer problem.

Choosing the right technology and skill sets to deliver your core customer journey is vital. In the initial phase of your startup, your reason for existence is to get your customers to love the product you have made. It is unlikely you will do this the first time around. You will need to modify your product several times or even radically alter it before your target customers take to it. YouTube started as a dating app. Instagram started as an app to post your location on social media. Most of the iconic tech companies today started life as something completely different. However, they had one thing in common; they were able to tweak or radically change their offer until customers started adopting their product. This meant they had the right technology to adapt quickly and cost-effectively. This should be the most important reason driving technology choices and design in the early stages of a startup. If you run out of money before you have delivered a product that customers want to adopt, it is game over before you have built the right thing.

The Three Key Technology Platforms You Need

There are essentially three types of technology platforms that you need to focus on to make good decisions from the onset.

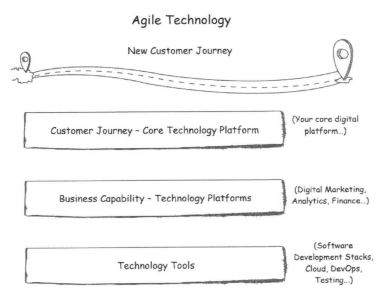

Agile Technology

New Customer Journey

Customer Journey – Core Technology Platform   (Your core digital platform...)

Business Capability – Technology Platforms   (Digital Marketing, Analytics, Finance...)

Technology Tools   (Software Development Stacks, Cloud, DevOps, Testing...)

Customer Journey – Core Technology Platforms

Your digital solution's reason for existence is the customer. This is the platform that customers will interact with to perform their main journey in a delightful manner. Amazon's core digital platform is its e-commerce software, which allows customers to choose and buy a product online and pay for it. Every other Amazon system is supporting this core customer journey platform.

The core customer journey platform is yours. This is what delivers the delightful journey that we have engineered so far in our blueprint. It explicitly and sometimes silently delivers that new, radically improved customer journey that the rest of the market isn't offering. As such, this is the one platform you need to get right first.

Once you have got past the prototype stage, this core platform needs to be engineered using the right technology tools so that it gives you agility. Building in agility from the onset means you can make rapid, cost-effective changes as required to improve your product and increase customer adoption.

Just after the prototype stage you need to select the right technology stack on which to engineer your core customer journey platform. These are tools such as programming language, databases, and software management tools required to build your working solution.

This is where the many choices can become overwhelming. Passionate arguments for using the Java language versus Python, and PostgreSQL versus MySQL databases will be commonplace. Remember, the key considerations here are delivering your future-proofed customer journey platform quickly and cost-effectively. We will dive deeper into the technology stack later in the chapter.

Business Capability – Technology Platforms

Business capability platforms are supporting systems to run and grow your venture. This involves marketing your product, gathering data and insights, managing your finances, and everything else that is required to operate your business.

In my view you don't need these when you are in the early stages of changing your solution to fit customer needs. These supporting platforms become more important when you have found your product-customer fit and are starting to see customer traction.

You need to understand that these support systems are efficiency drivers. They help you to lower the costs of acquiring and keeping customers, and doing your finances. They don't contribute towards growth if your core platform isn't delighting customers. In fact, if your core platform manages to delight customers, you will achieve organic growth through word of mouth marketing and will require little or no digital marketing or customer service systems.

Once you get to the scale-up stage, these business capability platforms can fuel your growth. If engineered correctly, you can achieve phenomenal growth with very little marginal cost per new customer.

Technology Tools

There is a myriad of internet technologies out there on which to build your platforms, but which do you choose? If you posed this question to any hands-on developer, they would give you a variety of answers favoring their preferred technology stack. However, the answer will almost always be one from the perspective of a business benefit and not an end-customer benefit. Yet ironically, almost every new technology, be it cloud, mobile, or DevOps emerged to solve an end-user problem. They often incidentally solved a business or developer problem as well, but this wasn't the aim. If these tools didn't help serve end-customers better, ultimately these tools failed. This isn't immediately obvious unless you had deep industry insights and watched the market evolve over time. Again, when we understand the technology stack and relate it to the customer experience we want to create, it is easier to zoom in on the right technology stack. I will explain this through a simple framework.

One of the basic things taught in any computer engineering course is the Open System Interconnection (OSI) model. The OSI model doesn't perform any functions in the computer networking process; it is a conceptual framework. I've adapted the framework to make sense of the various technologies of the internet.

Let's first understand what each of these layers does, then we will focus on what technology is relevant within each category.

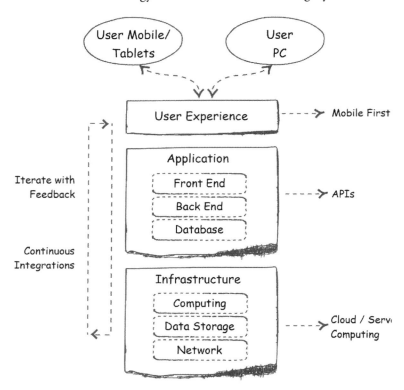

User Experience

Your solution needs to work seamlessly on everyday devices such as PCs, tablets, and mobiles without a glitch. Consumers now use multiple devices across one journey. Many journeys start on mobiles and finish on a tablet or PC, but the user doesn't think of their journey as being broken up across devices. As such, we need to design a seamless user experience even if the user is switching devices. The current focus, with good rationale, is to design applications for mobile devices first. Then this can scale across any device and provide a consistent experience.

The next layer is concerned with the user experience. This is your presentation layer, which displays your app in an appealing way across any device, bringing to life the new experience you have designed in the ideal customer journey. It isn't a technical layer done by a front-end developer, rather a user experience created by a designer.

Application Technology Stack

The next layer is the application. This is the code that delivers your new solution, contains your business logic, and stores and handles data associated with your app. The application layer consists of three sublayers:

- Front-end stack
- Back-end stack
- Databases

The front-end tech stacks are programming tools used to deliver the client side or what the user sees and interacts with.

Back-end tech stacks are programming tools used to execute your business logic on the servers that process them. This is unseen by the end user but is essentially the logic, or the brain, which orchestrates your customer journey. The user experience layer takes all its command from the back end based on what the user is doing. This is where the 'brain' processes various sets of data to deliver the customer journey.

Databases are used to store your application's data. These could be pre-required data that is needed to run your app, or data generated by users during their interaction with your app.

The combination of front-end tools, back-end tools and databases are referred to as the application technology stack or tech stack.

There are different specific framework technologies for each of these layers, and new ones emerge often. Frameworks are essentially components that help developers do mundane tasks easily and focus on the real value-adding work. As an example, user login management is used in every app and there are frameworks that provide components to manage this aspect without having to write code from scratch. Examples of front-end frameworks are React.js and Angular.

js, and examples of back-end development frameworks are Ruby on Rails, Symphony, and Django. These frameworks make working with Ruby, PHP and Python programming languages easier respectively.

In the Resources section at the end of this chapter, I've provided links to some good summary articles that compare the technology stacks generally used by tech startups.

Given the various different technology stacks that you can use to build your app, you will probably hear quite different advice from your tech partners. I've learnt over time that tech people naturally promote the languages and tools they are most familiar with. To filter this and determine the right technology stack for the job at hand, I have priorities for each sublayer depending on the application that needs to be built to deliver the customer journey.

On the front end, it is all about mobile compatibility and a fast, intuitive app experience for the users. At the same time, we want to maintain one set of code for all devices as much as possible, rather than having to maintain different codes for Apple, Android, or web browsers. As recently as the early 2010s, designing apps for multiple devices was a nightmare, and testing apps across devices was an even greater challenge. So, the industry set about solving the problem by standardizing smartphone browsers and operating systems, as well as creating software frameworks specifically suited for mobile app development. The objective here is to allow developers to focus on creating solutions and spend less time on testing across multiple devices. Here every tech business is trying to achieve this mobile-first outcome, so good front-end developers are highly sought after. This means developer costs are not your primary deciding factor.

On the back end, I look for the most developer-friendly framework that gives developers speed. They can then focus on creating your customer journey, rather than working on mundane tasks that the framework can take care of. Here, frameworks such as Ruby on Rails, and Symphony can offer great value.

The database layer has several open source options such as MySQL, Postgres, or MongoDB. Modern software architects are moving towards NoSQL technology, such as MongoDB. NoSQL databases were created to address the limitations of relational database technology such as MySQL. NoSQL databases support faster app development, removing the need to update the database structure as your app changes. They are more scalable and provide superior performance too. This agility is vital as you evolve your app to get customer traction.

As you select your technology stack, you need to be aware of some key trends in application development. These trends are driven by commercial considerations, and adapting to these trends can ensure the long-term vitality of your venture.

One of the challenges with software development has always been business growth, which inevitably causes software complexity, and maintenance and upgrades become difficult. To solve this inflexibility, the practice of writing code as self-contained blocks or modules emerged; these modules can be easily swapped out and replaced. These became known as microservices, where an application is structured as a collection of loosely coupled services. A key benefit of deconstructing an application into its component services is that it makes it easier and faster to change both the component and the overall application. This makes the application easier for developers to understand, build on, and test. In essence, we get agility and the business can on-board new software developers faster, as they can be assigned specific, small components, which they quickly become familiar with. Practically, this can represent a labor cost saving to the business.

In the same way microservices breaks down into its components, entire applications and businesses can be defined at a software level as Application Programming Interfaces (APIs). This technology alone truly allows you to create your business as a platform. Forward-thinking startups are building entire businesses as API-based platforms. So, why is this useful? APIs enable relevant authorized partners to interact with your applications and get the output. These partners can simply read the API documentation you create to learn how to make use of your application. The reason API platforms have taken off goes back to our economic principle of specialize and trade. Each platform can specialize in their core business service, and now they can trade that specialty with suitable partners. Prior to APIs, the cost of integrating with each partner made such an exercise unviable.

Today, a consumer looking for car insurance uses a comparison website such as confused.com. Once the user has input their information, the comparison website then calls the APIs of the various insurers to obtain a real-time quote. When the user selects an insurer, APIs from the comparison website passes the information back to the insurer. This happens within seconds with hundreds of insurers for just one insurance quote. This choice for the customer wouldn't have been possible without APIs.

While your business may not be ready to operate as a platform, it is sound to build it using APIs where possible. In the long term this will open up opportunities with partners, but in the short term you need your core customer journey platform to work seamlessly with the supporting applications. Integrating applications is much easier when they are API-based. Moreover, the proliferation of Software as a Service (SaaS) applications with API integration capability means you have significant choice on leveraging supporting platforms to scale your business.

The Cloud – Infrastructure as a Service

Beneath your app layer sits the infrastructure layer, which consists of three sublayers: computing power, data, and network.

Computing power allows you to run your apps. The more users you have on your app, the more computing power you will need even if there isn't a linear relationship.

You then have the data to be stored to run your app. This could be core data or real-time data produced by the users themselves, which runs the app and creates the customer experiences. You need to store, clean, and make the data available for your apps and supporting applications to use.

In the final sublayer, you have the network, which carries data between your apps and the external world.

Not too long ago, anyone who was building internet applications had to worry about the hardware and software to cater for the computing, data, and network elements of the infrastructure. Cloud technology has revolutionized the infrastructure part of app development. Today, infrastructure can be provisioned with cloud providers such as AWS, Microsoft Azure, and Google Cloud Platform instantly and with ease. Typically, you pay only for the computing resources used and scale infinitely without worrying about hardware, operating systems, and their ongoing management or costs. This development itself has now made it possible for bootstrapped startups to have the same access to computing power as the largest, cash rich organizations. This emergence of cloud computing has turned hardware and basic operating systems into services that can be accessed from anywhere. It is difficult to fully appreciate the benefits of cloud technology if you have not experienced managing hardware and operating systems the hard way before the cloud era. You now have infinite computing power that can be used as needed and turned off just with lines of code. This frees up developers' time to solve customer challenges.

The most basic category of cloud computing services is Infrastructure as a Service (IaaS). Here you rent IT infrastructure—servers and virtual machines, storage, networks, and operating systems from a cloud provider on a usage basis.

Platform as a Service (PaaS) refers to cloud computing services that provide an on-demand environment for building, testing, deploying, and managing software applications. PaaS exists to make web software development easier and faster for developers without worrying about setting up or managing the underlying servers, storage, network, and databases needed.

A key trend in PaaS is serverless computing. It focuses on building application functionality without any consideration for virtual machines or storage. The developer simply pays when their code runs. The cloud provider handles the setup, capacity planning, and server management for you. Serverless architectures are highly scalable and event-driven, only using resources when a specific function is used.

Agility Through Continuous Integration

A common pitfall that startup teams fall into is the whole team inadvertently becoming software testers. As everyone is vested in releasing a great product and would be embarrassed if customers found bugs, the team drifts towards testing, to ensure the whole product works every time new features are released. This becomes worse when they find bugs in new releases and do even more testing at every release. It has a downward spiraling effect. I've seen many startup entrepreneurs trying to release new features based on customer feedback get bogged down in testing and bug-fixing things, which were fixed in earlier releases.

Software development professionals recognized this was a severe form of waste. It not only wasted the team's time, but new releases became ever more difficult to deliver. Instead of releasing software quickly, the teams actually slowed down. This almost always ensured that such businesses couldn't scale. If they did, costs outpaced profits and sent the business under. The software industry came up with several tools, processes, and behavior changes to address this. These are now known as Continuous Integration and Continuous Delivery, more commonly known as CI-CD.

Today, CI-CD is the central pillar of software development agility. Companies that truly adopt CI-CD practices release software daily or even by the minute. Let's understand how they do this.

Developers practicing continuous integration (CI) merge changes to the existing code as often as possible. The developer's changes are verified by first building the new version and running pre-designed tests against this new version. By doing this, you avoid the integration challenges and bugs that happen when large pieces of the new code are added to existing code. If the new code didn't work as intended, or it introduces bugs in the overall software, this can be corrected quickly, and the integration relaunched. This creates confidence in developers that they have not inadvertently broken something and increases their productivity. For this approach to work, developers need to adopt the practice of writing automated test cases for every piece of work they produce, known as Test-Driven Development (TDD). This is required for the CI tools to deliver the benefits. CI focuses on testing automation to check that the application isn't broken whenever new code is integrated into the main codebase.

Continuous delivery (CD) is an extension of continuous integration to ensure that you can release software changes to your customers quickly over the long term. On top of having automated your testing, you have also automated your release process, which involves releasing your software to the right place without undoing previous work. However, the final process of pushing the latest version live to customers is still done by a human. With CD, you can release daily, weekly, fortnightly, or as you choose. However, to benefit from CD, you should deploy to live as often as possible to ensure you release small batches that are easy to troubleshoot and fix in case of problems.

You can go a step further and push releases to live automatically. This is known as continuous deployment. However, you may not need this level of automation in the early stages when you are trying to get to the customer traction stage. Once you have reached this stage, continuous deployment could become more relevant.

Once you are past the prototype stage of your product, it is highly useful to ensure all your coding is developed using the CI-CD process. It is worth the slight extra effort developers need to put into this at the onset to reap the ongoing returns.

In the Resources section of this chapter, I've provided links to a summary of continuous integration and continuous delivery tools, which you will find useful.

A Simple Method to Filter the Technology Noise

We have looked at the three key technology areas as customer journey platforms, business capability platforms, and technology stacks.

If there are only these three areas you need to be concerned about, why are there so many technologies out there? And a new one with its own acronym seems to come around every other day. If we look at why these technologies are evolving it is much easier to make sense of them.

Almost all of the internet technologies and tools today have come about to solve one of three challenges associated with the explosive growth of the internet. From 1994 to 2018, the internet has had 4.4 billion users, and as of 2018, one million new users each day use the internet. There has never been a bigger phenomenon in the history of humanity.

The technologies that power the internet have developed rapidly to keep up with this growth in demand.

Whatever the technology, they have all evolved to:

- Improve end user experience
- Increase software agility
- Make it easier for software developers to build better software, faster and cheaper

The growth of smartphones and the 'always on the internet' user meant that what emerged as a desktop-based software had to radically change to provide a compelling experience on a small-screen device. This drove the development of front-end-focused frameworks such as Angular.js and Reat.js These frameworks made developing for a variety of mobile devices easier to manage and provided a better experience for end users while using the apps. This development has driven an explosive growth in mobile and app adoption.

The second driver for the proliferation of new tools and technologies is the need to swiftly improve software, based on the new features and changes the end users demanded. Software teams could no longer rely on old waterfall methods where they went through an analyze-build-test-release cycle. They could no longer deliver in six-month release cycles. Instead, software teams had to do all of these activities in parallel and repeat them frequently on an almost daily or weekly basis. Amazon engineers deploy code every 11.7 seconds, on average, reducing both the number and duration of outages at the same time. Netflix engineers deploy code thousands of times per day. This need for agility led to the development of the continuous integration or DevOps idea, where software testing and integration is automated and continuous. The significance of this is that software developers can focus on adding and optimizing features and reacting to customer demand, as opposed to spending time on testing and release management.

The third driver is to help software developers build better software faster and cheaper. The rocketing demand for skilled software talent meant that wages went up dramatically. Every business had an internet-related initiative, and demand outstripped supply. This made technology resources relatively expensive, so organizations tried to get the most out of these resources. Software languages emerged that were easier to learn and use, like Microsoft's .NET, ColdFusion, and Python, all of which reduce the learning curve and make development easier. This meant that developers could now teach themselves rather than having a computer science degree; it democratized access to building software. At the same time, simpler Integrated Development Environments (IDEs) to build software, repositories for multiple developers to collaborate (GitHub), and other such tools emerged to make life easier for developers.

You can place most of the internet technologies under one of the above three categories. This will then help you understand what tools are useful to you as your startup takes shape and grows. All of the above technology is there to help developers be more productive in solving end-user challenges. Don't lose sight of this perspective.

In determining your ideal tech stack, you will hear lots of debates over which programming language is better. There is no clear winner. It all depends on what you are trying to achieve. There are two questions you can ask to figure out which programming language is best suited for your mission. Firstly, what is the availability of skill sets? Here you need to think of long-term availability of skill sets in your geographic area if you are setting up base there and will be building your internal engineering capabilities as you scale. This first question will often narrow down the candidate software languages. Ensure the languages you have in your shortlist all have an extensive pool of talent. Avoid languages sought after by large corporations, such as Java, as there is a narrower pool of talent and, as a result, they are more expensive. At the same time, don't pick languages that are niche and don't have a large number of developers working on them.

Secondly, can the language preferred by your candidates deliver the customer journey platform now and in the future? It would help to share your blueprint at this stage to help the candidates understand what you are trying to do. One technique that has worked well for me is to set the candidates an assignment to compare two languages that are best suited to deliver the customer journey platform. This can be an informative exercise to help select the language, as well as the candidate.

How to Develop Your Product

Now that you have an appreciation of the key technologies, you need to work with your tech team to get your venture off the ground, and you need to be clear about how you build your product. More importantly, who do you work with in order to build and continuously develop your product? Again, entrepreneurs have struggled with clarity on this through no fault of their own. The ever-growing noise around how various unicorns have built their technology leads them to make decisions that are not grounded in the fundamental economics of the software labor market.

Many entrepreneurs go down the route of building everything internally all the time. This group cites full control over their intellectual property and speed as key reasons for this. At the other extreme, some outsource all their work to external parties. This group cites perceived cost savings and availability of expertise as their driver. Both struggle at various stages and often fall out with their tech teams, and the startup is derailed.

As with all things, there is a season for each approach. In my view, a mixed approach taking into account where the startup is in on its journey can help align interest between the various parties and lead to successful ongoing product development.

Observing the numerous projects and technology agencies I've worked with, I started to understand the economic drivers behind the failure and success of software building; two forces shape the success or failure of software engineering initiatives.

Firstly, demand for software talent outstrips supply in most of the developed world. This has a strong influence on what capabilities are available to a startup, whether it is well funded or not.

Secondly, money doesn't solve the talent problem, unlike most other economic challenges. Whether you are outsourcing or building an internal team to develop your product, the availability of a talent ecosystem and long-term interest alignment are key to getting from prototype stage to a wildly successful business.

The above two dynamics cause all sorts of challenges to the entrepreneur, not least of which is spending, and perhaps wasting, precious capital on expensive tech mercenaries. This happens more often than we imagine, due to the demand for talent outstripping supply. Part of the inspiration for creating my agile digital strategy blueprint and writing this book was to help entrepreneurs to avoid wasting resources on working with expensive talent, who are not necessarily aligned on interests.

The approach that works well is to:

1. Create your agile digital strategy blueprint to reach clarity and get buy-in on your vision and goals.
2. Leverage talent across the market by outsourcing your prototype build with skilled specialist agencies. This gives you access to a talent pool that is interested in creating cool products. Get this agency team aligned with your vision using the blueprint. Topcoder and similar marketplaces are good places to leverage a global talent pool to develop your products.
3. When you have beta launched and proved that your product has customer traction, continue to work with external providers but start to augment the work with a small internal team.
4. As you scale and grow gradually, transition fully to an internal team that continuously builds and develops the core journey platform.
5. At the scale-up stage you will need additional business capability technology platforms. In most cases, you can buy these platforms as services and get your internal team to integrate with your core journey platforms.

This approach is summarized in the diagram below.

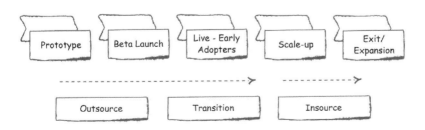

There are good reasons for insourcing or outsourcing at the various stages of your startup's growth.

During the prototype stage you want to create a sufficiently engaging solution for your potential customers to feedback on. At this stage, if you get your prototype wrong, the chances of customers rejecting your solution are high. As such, there is too much at stake for you to bet the future of your startup on a few people who can make or break your prototype. Getting as many people to work on different prototypes that you can test against your customer base is a better bet. However, with your limited resources you don't have the luxury of trying different teams or agencies. With the agile digital strategy blueprint in hand, you have already taken steps to clarify your idea on what needs to be built, why, and for whom. You cannot underestimate the power of this tool because the alternative is that you spend lots of time and effort, at your own expense, trying to create and clarify the idea and communicate it to people who will build you a prototype. This can be an enormously expensive and frustrating exercise. However, with the blueprint in hand you can actually create a competition for software developers to build the prototype for you. You can use a website such as Topcoder (https://www.topcoder.com) to create and run a crowdsourcing competition to build a prototype. This way you can access a global talent pool to work on your challenge and create a solution exceeding your expectations.

In 2018, I undertook a similar exercise for a large retailer in the UK. This retailer ran a successful global, e-commerce operation in the health and wellness space. They needed help to select their next generation e-commerce system, as well as to select the system integrator required to deliver the new solution. The retailer faced an interesting conundrum. They had a long list of system integrators, who they'd worked with in the past, all of whom were very keen to pitch for this new work. Selecting a system integrator based on a paper proposal wasn't going to work, as they were all of a similar caliber. To make the most of the situation, I created an interesting process where we invited all seven eligible system integrators to submit brief proposals, but then shortlisted three of them to build a prototype in a three-day hackathon.

The hackathon was designed to not only test the technical abilities of the system integrators but also reveal the ways in which they would work to deliver the actual project. At the end of the three-day hackathon, the teams presented their output and were judged by a panel of 15 people from across the business. It was a highly useful process because at the end of the three days there was a working prototype, and decisions on the selection could be made on objective criteria. Interestingly, the three system integrators found this innovative process very motivating and gave their very best as a team to win.

Software developers and design agencies thrive on solving interesting challenges in innovative ways. This is what wins them future business. As such, knowing how to leverage this motivation can help you build the right product quickly. As a young startup you wouldn't yet be able to attract the best talent, so having the agile digital strategy blueprint ready, and by leveraging competitive instincts through crowdsourcing, can help you get your prototype from global talent.

When they have found the right agencies to kickstart their products, entrepreneurs then make the mistake of continuing to work with the same agency when they have achieved customer traction. This usually doesn't end well. Firstly, the agency that was good at designing your prototype may not have the right skill set fit to continuously develop your platform, which needs to grow with customers. During the growth phase, deep understanding of the core customer journey platform is key to being able to continuously improve the platform quickly. As new customers use the platform, key improvements need to be delivered to it to keep delighting existing customers and attracting new ones. So, the velocity of product enhancements needs to keep pace with the customer growth. If not, you will find a nimbler competitor will offer a better solution and quickly overtake you.

When you have steady customer traction, it is the right time for you to start building internal software engineering capabilities to work on your customer journey platforms. You can go through a transition phase where your internal engineers work with your external agencies to increasingly bring the development of the product in-house. By augmenting the agency with your engineers, you will increase product release cycle, as well as build up valuable tacit knowledge within your team to continuously understand and cater for customer needs. There is enormous value in this. This is what drives long-term growth and the value of your business.

As your business matures and your brand becomes established in the market, you will be able to attract valuable talent to join your business far more easily. This is a good time for you to cherry-pick talent and build an even better team. As the business matures, and if you are considering any exit, the value of an internal engineering team for the company is simply unquestionable.

The internet has truly been a phenomenon that has flipped many entrenched ideas on their heads and created completely new trillion-dollar businesses in record time, while decimating others. Before the internet, as companies and industries grew, it became ever more difficult to enter these markets or disrupt incumbents, as they built ever higher barriers to entry. The internet has changed this. Today you have the same access to the technologies, almost for free, which the largest corporations have. Knowledge of and access to these technologies have been democratized. You have the tools to disrupt any industry you choose. In fact, you have too many tools.

The purpose of this chapter has been to demystify the tools available to you. We have done this through conceptual frameworks. By simplifying your platforms into customer journey platforms, business capability platforms, and technology stacks, you now appreciate the role of these in your various phases as you develop your product. Importantly, using the right technology stack gives you the agility required to get customer traction and scale beyond that.

You now also understand when to insource or outsource your software engineering and the economic drivers behind that.

The most valuable thing you will have learnt by now is to connect the thread between your ideal customer journey, which your team understands and is aligned behind, and the tech solution that will help you deliver it.

Resources

There is a blog post that provides an easy to understand summary of technology stacks. Various different technology stacks are introduced without the jargon.

https://tms-outsource.com/blog/posts/technology-stack/

Another blog post compares the modern web development frameworks and languages.

https://tms-outsource.com/blog/posts/web-technologies/

Topcoder is a crowdsourcing platform with an open global community of designers, developers, data scientists, and competitive programmers. It pays community members for their work on the projects and sells community services to startups and corporate clients. Topcoder can be good way for you to design, prototype, or develop your app.

https://www.topcoder.com/

Udacity is an offshoot of free computer science classes offered in 2011 through Stanford University. It offers a combination of free technology courses and nanodegrees focused on developing skill sets in specific areas. Classes are taught online in an interactive manner. Udacity is a great place to pick up some technical skills or get an appreciation of a subject area.

Every once in a while, a new technology, an old problem, and a big idea turn into an innovation.

~ Dean Kamen ~

Chapter 7

GovTech Singapore – Moments of Life

On August 9, 1965, the leader of a small state in South-East Asia addressed his citizens in a televised address. He had bad news. On that same day, members of the Malaysian parliament had unanimously voted to expel Singapore from the Malaysian Federation. Anyone witnessing the televised speech on that day would have agreed that this event ended any prospect of Singapore surviving. The Cambridge-educated Lee Kuan Yew, who was delivering the speech, understood the gravity of the situation. He broke down in tears as he addressed his citizens.

For readers who are not familiar with the geography, Malaysia is located in South-East Asia and has a land mass of 330,000 square kilometers, roughly the same size as Japan. Singapore is located at the southern tip of Malaysia, separated by a channel, and has a land area of just 720 square kilometers, which in 1965 housed a tiny population of just 1.9 million people. Singapore has no natural resources other than a deep harbor and its strategic geographic location at the tip of the Malaysian Peninsular, a commanding position for many shipping routes. The British, who colonized the country in 1819, saw its potential as a harbor and trading port, and developed Singapore as a trading hub. This caused an influx of Chinese and Indian immigrants, who settled along with the indigenous Malays. With its tiny land area, surrounded by the seas, and with zero natural resources, Singapore had no chance of feeding its population if the motherland, Malaysia, kicked it out of its federation. That is exactly the situation in which Singapore found itself in 1965.

Fast forwarding just 50-odd years, Singapore is an economic miracle. It has one of the highest per capita incomes at US$58,000 per year as of 2018, on a par with the US and higher than many resource-rich countries. It has the highest home ownership rate, with 91.2% of its people owning their homes. On education, health, environment, or any other metric, Singapore consistently tops the charts. A country which, by most reasoning, should not have survived, has truly beaten the odds and has become an example of progress and success. It is thriving today.

So, when I came to know of Singapore's Moments of Life (MOL) digital initiative, what would have surprised many others who are not familiar with Singapore didn't really surprise me. The sheer boldness of the MOL digital initiative, its vision, customer focus, and brilliant execution are how things are usually done in Singapore, even though outsiders may find it extraordinary. It is in Singapore's very DNA to be doing such an extraordinary thing.

I became aware of MOL while I was writing this book; at the time it didn't cross my mind to feature it as an integrative case study here. This is perhaps because MOL is a government initiative. However, on understanding MOL better, it seemed a perfect fit as an example of an organization putting everything we've learned into practice. At its heart it is an entrepreneurial venture, even if it is funded by the Singapore government.

MOL is a digital initiative launched by the Government Technology Agency of Singapore, also known as GovTech, which executes the government technology and digital strategy. It also acts as the coordinator of technology and digital services for all government agencies in Singapore who provide services to citizens. In some cases, GovTech builds digital services for other agencies.

Singapore's government has prioritized technology as a core driver of its economy in the 21st century. Given this direction, various government agencies have embraced digital transformation and made many of their services available online. From applying for passports, to filing taxes, or buying a flat, most government services, if not all, can be accessed online. To facilitate secure access, Singapore introduced SingPass secure single sign-on as early as 2003. With just a single username and password, coupled with a secure two-factor authentication system, citizens can access any government service securely. Given such ease of use, adoption of government e-services was already amongst the highest in the world. Not being content with such an achievement, and to continually improve, GovTech launched its MOL initiative in 2018.

GovTech understood that citizens would try to access a government service, for example to pay taxes or apply for a passport, at the time they needed that service. This was fine and it already worked well. However, what if the government mapped the entire lifetime journey of a citizen and ensured they obtained the right services, at the right time, based on their life situation? GovTech figured that if it mapped the journey from cradle to grave and ensured that digital services would be available across their entire lifetime in a relevant and timely manner, it could save citizens time, hassle, effort, and ultimately improve their quality of life. Citizens could then focus on other economic, value-adding activities or leisure, rather than filling forms or worrying about not fulfilling a mandatory task at the right time. Improving the quality of life of its citizens should be the prime motivation of any government, but it is rare these days to witness this when we scan the globe. It is so refreshing to see Singapore aspire to this relentlessly.

Dominic Chan is the director in charge of the MOL platform and is responsible for its strategy and roll-out. I met him in London in early 2019 to prepare this case study. This is what Dominic told me:

> Citizens were not benchmarking government digital services with other governments. They never were, but increasingly they expect the same level of value and usability, which they experience every day from companies such as Google, Amazon, or Uber. While the government isn't in competition with these commercial solutions, citizens are unconsciously comparing digital experiences.

> Moments of Life is an initiative to map our citizens' journeys. There are 102 government agencies in Singapore. Citizens interact with some of these agencies at some point in their life. There may not be suitable awareness amongst citizens on where they need to go to or when. Of the 102 agencies, some are well known but many are not.

Amongst the agencies there may be useful schemes to upskill and train, or obtain certain assistance, but the citizen may be unaware of their existence. MOL aims to be the citizen's digital concierge and a single point of access.

One will be able to log in with their SingPass and, once logged in, the MOL app will take the citizen to a personalized screen with relevant services for the citizen, based on their life situation. This will save users time, hassle, and effort, and we hope it will deepen interactions between citizens and government agencies. Our ambition is to ensure all government digital services are available through the MOL platform. Not just through its own central app, but through any government website. For example, a young person who is going through education would mostly interact with the Ministry of Education and its agencies. However, such a person may also be interacting with another government agency, such as the Ministry of Health. Regardless of which government agency the citizen interacts with, relevant information and services should be available based on their life stage and situation.

Our plans are to expand the MOL initiative to the business sector. We believe that, just like a citizen's journey through life, businesses also go through different stages in their journey. Today, Singapore already provides various digital services for businesses, from setting up to filing taxes. Similar to MOL for citizens, we envisage a digital concierge for businesses. Through this concierge, businesses can interact with government digital services, based on their present situation, and have access to the right service at the right time in one single place. This will lower businesses' compliance and administrative costs, hassle, and time. It will allow them to focus on their core business activities, hopefully making a positive impact on their customers and wider economy.

GovTech has taken an agile approach to the development and rollout of its MOL initiative. It is currently rolling out a minimum viable product of its digital concierge service for testing with actual users. At the same time, it is modernizing the technical architecture that provides these services. Its plan is to break down various services, such as applying for a passport or filing taxes, into small, component microservices. These microservices can then be rolled out to any agency website and the user need not visit multiple, specific websites to access a service.

If we analyze MOL in the context of the agile digital strategy blueprint, from its birth as part of a national digital transformation, to its agile implementation underpinned by a natural agile mindset, we can see that the strategy perfectly embodies the concepts set out in this book.

We embrace the idea of businesses competing amongst each other quite naturally. However, it isn't so natural for us to think of countries competing with each other. To those who have grown up in Singapore, the idea of countries competing amongst each other is quite a familiar concept. Children in Singapore are taught about its history and basic economic structure. Having rapidly developed its economy without any natural resources and purely based on the enterprise of its people, Singaporeans are quite comfortable with the idea of competition, both at a local and global level.

Singapore has a young generation that is growing up exposed to digital services and processes that are globally competitive in nature. These users expect the same level, if not better experience from government services as well. To compete for the mindshare of this younger generation, government services not only need to be digital, but also need to offer the best possible experience.

Singapore has constantly reinvented its economic structure to be ahead of its competitors, to attract the best multinational companies, capital, and talent. Post-independence, it focused on manufacturing activities, shipping, and petroleum. In more recent times, Singapore has moved into more value-added engineering and manufacturing, such as semiconductors and hard disks. It has also developed the financial, banking, and services sector to support its industries. Today, Singapore has emerged as the default choice for many multinational companies setting up their regional headquarters. Being at the center of the booming Asian economies such as China and India, Singapore is now reinventing itself as a hub for financial technology, digital innovations, and services. As such, Singapore is constantly competing with other centers, such as Hong Kong, London, and New York, to attract the best foreign investment and talent.

Its competitive advantage arises from its visionary and efficient government, clean environment, and overall quality of life for citizens. The Singapore government plays a major role in its economic development. While there is a thriving private sector, the government shapes economic policy for the long term and catalyzes development. It then puts in the necessary infrastructure for the needs of these industries. As an example, Singapore's economic vision in the early 2000s recognized that information technology would play a major part in the global economy, since the arrival of the internet. To support the internet industry, it encouraged the development of internet data centers, undersea cable linkages, as well as high-speed, fiber broadband throughout the country as early as the year 2000. As a result, the entire country has access to lightning-fast internet access.

Today the country is focused on the impact that digital transformation is having on various industries. To leverage the benefits of digital and emerging technologies, it has launched the smart nation strategy. Initiatives such as MOL are aimed at delivering the overall strategy.

The Singapore government has taken bold strides in its computerization and e-government journey since the 1980s. Today, Singapore's e-government efforts are well regarded internationally, and its people and businesses are able to transact with the government online, and public officers make use of digital tools in their daily work. The Singapore government believes the conditions are now ripe for it to take digital transformation to the next level. Rapid technological advances, particularly in big data, Internet of Things (IoT) and Artificial Intelligence (AI), have the potential to fundamentally transform the government for the better. Smart Nation is an overarching digital strategy to drive the next generation of government digital transformation.

Why do all this? This is Singapore's way of competing in the world market by providing first-class infrastructure, support services, and human capital for its businesses and citizens to thrive. From a bigger picture perspective, freeing up citizens' time and making necessary tasks as easy as possible, the initiative can release the energy of its people. In 2016, the Prime Minister of Singapore, Mr. Lee Hsien Long, summed it up well when he wished for every Singaporean to be 'gracefully discontented', where everyone competes against themselves for the betterment of society. This is an enlightened approach to competition, and one any business or country would do well to learn from.

From the concepts we have covered in the 'How Do You Compete?' chapter, it is apparent that looking at the entire lifetime journey of a citizen is a novel and bold take on the customer journey mapping approach. Moreover, MOL personas are defined by life stages, such as children, students, young families, matured families, and the older generation.

By eliminating unnecessary paperwork, while increasing convenience and speed through digitization, we can see the ERIC process in action. This is then overlaid on the MOL customer journey to ensure a far superior experience to that which citizens were used to before digitization.

Singapore not just plans well but executes brilliantly. I grew up in Singapore, moving there when I was five, and I lived there until my mid-thirties, when I moved to the UK. I visit family and friends every few years and the one thing that strikes me when I return is the pace of change. Almost everywhere I turn, things look new and different. New buildings and infrastructure are constructed in record time, new apps and digital services are adopted rapidly, and lifestyles change quickly. This isn't surprising, as the agile mindset is embedded in Singaporean culture. When digital services were offered as part of MOL, the rate of adoption by users was rapid.

From the internal mindset point of view, those who are working to deliver MOL understand the agile mindset quite intuitively. Interestingly, relative to other countries, you can find some of the most talented and driven people in the country working in Singapore's government sector. The sense of purpose of serving citizens, as well as the desire to be world class, embeds an agile mindset within GovTech teams.

The emphasis for mastery in digital and disruptive technologies comes right from the top. The Prime Minister of Singapore has taught himself to code, to get an appreciation of the subject. In his speeches on technology, that knowledge and understanding comes through and he resonates with even the most tech savvy audience. This appreciation for mastering subjects is now cascading through the nation and initiatives such as MOL.

In terms of building agile teams, GovTech has focused on developing technology capabilities amongst its citizens. This then allows it to form the agile teams it needs to deliver initiatives such as MOL. Singapore recognizes that deep technical and software engineering capabilities need to be mastered across disciplines such as AI, big data and IoT. GovTech is now actively engaged in building internal engineering capabilities in addition to augmenting skills from external partners. To drive its talent acquisition schemes, GovTech has been attracting Singaporeans who have been living abroad and working in the technology sector. This is in addition to upskilling and retraining its existing workforce.

Within GovTech, agile teams are set up to deliver products end to end. The approach is changing from delivering discrete projects to developing and improving products on a long-term basis. Agile, Scrum and kanban are adopted in its new product initiatives. There are daily scrums in the morning to share team progress and next steps. GovTech is also using 'pair programming', where each task is assigned two developers who share ideas and sometimes have 'intense' discussions before writing code.

As part of its transformation, GovTech is changing its underlying technology structure. Having managed disparate siloed systems, often supplied by competing vendors with little interest in collaboration, it has started to take ownership of the core of its systems. It has adopted the platform strategy where microservices are used to expose services through APIs. The platform named Application Programming Interface Exchange (APEX) allows GovTech's systems to easily 'talk' or to exchange information with the digital systems of other public agencies. This allows services such as SingPass single sign-on to be available across apps as an API. MOL itself is being constructed as microservices, so that any other apps that need to use one of MOL's services can access it without disrupting the user's journey.

In addition, GovTech is taking a cloud-first approach, where its new infrastructure and apps are cloud based. This breaks dependencies on hardware and operating systems, and gives software engineers the ability to turn off and on computing capacity using just code.

GovTech's Next-Generation Container Architecture, or NECTAR, is the platform providing the benefits and flexibility of cloud services, but with reduced operational and security concerns, and greater compliance with GovTech requirements.

As digital services become an integral part of everyday life, they have to be easy to use, adaptable, and relevant. Ideally, from a governance, security, and scalability point of view, various parties should develop their own applications independently but with compatibility in mind. To enable other government agencies to develop and deploy applications rapidly, GovTech is developing the Singapore Government Tech Stack (SGTS), a common platform that makes the process simpler and more streamlined. With SGTS, agencies will be able to use a suite of tools and services hosted on a common infrastructure to ensure consistency and high quality of their applications.

These new platforms are allowing GovTech's engineers to focus on problem solving through coding rather than sitting in meetings talking about interfaces with other systems.

MOL exemplifies the approach of seeking a competitive advantage by putting the customer at the heart of a solution design. It stands out for its boldness of mapping a person's life journey. This is the customer journey stretched to its maximum. GovTech's focus on an agile mindset, teams, and technology to execute the vision, sets it up to succeed. By adopting this same approach and the Agile Digital Strategy Blueprint we have covered here, you too can set your venture up to scale great heights.

Chapter 8
Conclusion

If you are reading these pages, you would have likely thought the content so far to be useful. It will be even more useful when you take action based on the knowledge and tools you now have. The agile digital strategy blueprint is your starting point to building the right thing. I've provided a template you can download at hajajdeen.com, which contains the various elements and templates of the blueprint. By thinking through and filling them out, you will make a great start in the right direction. You will be on your way to reaching clarity on the crucial questions of where and how your new venture is going to compete, and the resources you need in terms of mindset, teams, and technology.

As you work through the blueprint, engage your inner circle and domain experts you trust to give you feedback and help you refine your blueprint; you will be positively surprised how quickly your blueprint evolves into a viable plan to get your venture off the ground.

Taking the first step in any new initiative can be the hardest thing. Self-doubts, doubts from others, and confusion can all end initiatives before they even begin. The agile digital strategy blueprint has been designed to avoid false starts by prioritizing clarity and catalyzing the right resources around you, to not just get started in the right direction but to succeed in your mission.

In 2018, I collaborated with Paul at a large UK mortgage services business with annual revenues of £600 million. He had recently been recruited as the Chief Technology Officer and was a deep technical expert. He had an impressive CV, having worked with some of the biggest US technology companies. His mission was to use technology both to deliver cost efficiencies and the business's expansion strategy. Paul jumped straight into his role and recruited an internal engineering team, moving away from the outsourced technology partners the business had been working with until then.

He recruited an impressive team of engineers and engineering managers. Fast forward six months and a new CEO arrived at the business. Paul was unable to show much value in terms of his team's output, even though the business's costs had gone up significantly as a result of a setting up a new engineering function.

One of Paul's major failings in this scenario was that he focused on technology; his area of expertise, his comfort zone. He failed to see the bigger picture, the context under which the business was operating, and how it could compete in its niche. In the space in which this mortgage business was playing, new digital disruptors were starting up AI-based robo-advisors on mortgages with significantly lower fees. Customers were starting to adopt these digital disruptors, as their new journey with these disruptors was significantly improved compared to the clumsy websites of traditional mortgage services. Had Paul and his team worked through in a structured manner, perhaps using my blueprint, they would have picked the right initiatives that would have added value. Had Paul been a business executive, he would have focused on the strategy and missed the technology. That too would have failed.

Hence, the mission of this book: getting to a position of clarity in a simple visual way that both you and those around you understand. That clarity is vital for you to be aligned as a team and to go on to succeed. You already have the blueprint tool in your hand to use and get started.

In my own experience, having a simple visual tool to systematically take your audience through can be extremely valuable. It confers both clarity and credibility to your communications. It makes it easier for people to believe, and they do want to believe if you can present the right information in an easy to understand manner. When you do this right, and in a humble manner, engaging the audience to co-create with you, the response can truly be inspiring.

A clear mind is like a magnet. It only attracts the right ideas, people, and resources to get what it wants done. The agile digital strategy blueprint helps to get to clarity as well as acting as that magnet around which your ideas, people, and resources converge.

As you dtoesign your new solution, the most important consideration is your customer and the value you are providing. It is easy to lose sight of this. So, keep in mind your target customer journey map. Perhaps make this visible in your team's workspace by having a large copy prominently displayed. Constantly having your team review its progress against the customer journey can give you real measures of progress.

You are not just designing an organization for your customers; the people who make your business what it is must also have great fun doing it. At the end of the day, it really is about people. If you have a delighted team, you will more than likely have a delighted and growing customer base as well.

As you go through your journey there will be challenges; that is inevitable. The knowledge you have accumulated and the planning you have done through the blueprint sets you up to navigate those challenges and go on to succeed. At the end of every challenge is growth. Your agile mindset rooted in your true purpose will keep you guided.

Build your team with this same mindset and energize them. Frame challenges in the context of the blueprint to keep yourself and your team motivated.

We have simplified technology for you. Remember, technology is an enabler to delight customers. You are in charge of it and not the other way around. Understanding evolving technology in its right context will help your team stay focused and prevent it becoming overwhelmed.

It is my hope that this book was useful to you and that it will positively impact on your next venture. It is my wish and blessing that you achieve success and grow during that process.

P.S. Please do connect with me on LinkedIn to stay in touch.

https://www.linkedin.com/in/hajajdeen/

Agile Digital Strategy Blueprint templates are available for free download at hajajdeen.com.

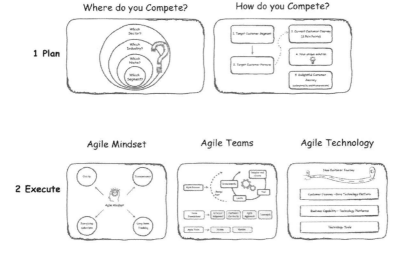

"Action is eloquence."

William Shakespeare